DON'T
ANSWER
EVERY
CALL

A Practical Approach to Relieve
Stress, Set Boundaries, & Take
Control of Your Life

FRANCIS GREENE

Disclaimer

This book is designed to provide information and motivation to our readers. It is sold with the understanding that the publisher is not engaged to render any type of psychological, legal, or any other kind of professional advice. The instructions, recommendations, and advice in this book are not intended as a substitute for professional counseling. The content of each chapter is the sole expression and opinion of its author. No warranties or guarantees are expressed or implied by the author's and publisher's choice to include any of the content in this volume. Neither the publisher nor the individual author shall be liable for any physical, psychological, emotional, financial, or commercial damages, including, but not limited to, special, incidental, consequential, or other damages. Our views and rights are the same:

You are responsible for your own decisions, choices, actions, and results.

Publisher

DEDICATION

Ervin Greene Jr.

If the essence you found
was spread throughout the world,
It would be a better place.
Not financially better,
not materially better,
not intellectually better,
JUST BETTER.

You Captured Your Mindful Moments.

CONTENTS

Part One: The Mindful Moment

Part Two: Insufficient Coverage

Part Three: I Already Answered

Part Four: Premium Alternatives

Part Five: Better Impact

ACKNOWLEDGEMENTS

I would like to express heartfelt gratitude and appreciation to J. Tucker, J. Kennedy, and E. Goad for being perceptive enough to notice, patient enough to endure, and courageous enough to introduce me to my Self. Through your selflessness and grace, you revealed a presence that was concealed within, encouraged me to embrace it, and challenged me to present my true self to the world. The work you do every day through touching the lives of those around you is more impactful than you could ever imagine. I am forever indebted and commit to continue paying it forward.

INTRODUCTION

"There are certain people who definitely are more influenced by their surroundings than by their own intentions. While there are other people who are more influenced by the subjective factor." -Carl Jung

Carl Jung introduced the world to introverted and extroverted personality types in the early twentieth century, but he made the quoted statement above during a later interview when questioned about these familiar personality types. While some people are more influenced by external activity, everyone receives influence from their environment through sense perceptions and interpretations of their surroundings. If the external influence we receive can overpower our own intentions as Jung stated in this quote, how much does that external influence affect our thinking, perceptions, mood, behavior, and our ability to establish and maintain focus and clarity?

This question requires us to compare our intentions to the activities we actually fulfill on any given day. If they don't align, we need to explore what is actually guiding our lives. If we objectively investigate our habits, routines, and our pursuit of the goals we struggle to meet, we might discover instances in which we directly act against our intentions. We may find that our failure to carry out many of our intentions is indeed inspired by environmental influences.

No one steps into the day seeking self-sabotage, yet we often find ourselves neglecting our best intentions and pursuing random, but captivating ideas. As each idea approaches, we have the option to ignore the call or engage in it. However, if the idea is presented in a way that touches your awareness, it may be difficult to ignore.

Marketing departments and public relations experts target and strategically present some influence to create that emotional connection. These interruptions create pathways to alternative interests that prevent us from focusing on our intentions. We reorganize our priorities to incorporate these new concepts, and our original intentions become secondary.

In the following chapters, we will explore the dilemma we face when welcoming and embracing calls that are influencing our lives and interrupting our intentions. We'll see the importance and the drawbacks of acknowledging every call to our consciousness and the impact of the ideas we unintentionally accept and store in our minds every day. They are the aspects that are elevating or undermining our lives. We will discover new ways to hear everything, but also how to impartially differentiate between what we should accept, allow, and reject from external sources and from our internal stockpile of ideas and beliefs.

This book is for the imperfectionist. That includes those among us who have made mistakes, miscalculations, missteps, and errors in judgment. It's for those that know we will continue to fall short of perfection but want to avoid damaging our lives further and hurting others along the way. Let's move forward to accept the challenges life is presenting with the confidence to face any uncertainty without hesitation.

"Although today may not be perfect,

It is where we start making things better."

Part One

The Mindful Moment

Chapter 1

It's Not the Call,
It's Your Answer

The Call

An unknown caller is reaching out to you.

He tells you he's a representative from your bank and informs you of a problem with your account. He warns you of the financial loss you'll suffer if you don't fix this issue during this call. He'll also be forced to suspend your account, leaving you without access to the remaining funds. He demands that you provide him with the necessary information to resolve the problem quickly.

After you've reluctantly given what he's asked, he informs you of his true intention. He's draining your account and will use your personal information to commit fraud. He suggests you prepare to deal with the hardship that will follow. Finally, he thanks you for your cooperation and apologizes for the shock, anger, and sadness heading your way.

It's rare for someone approaching you to offer this type of transparency. Instead, strangers, friends, and even loved ones don't reveal their true intent until after you've given your time, money, energy, heart, or something else valuable. Then, you're left with the suffering, self-doubt, and the difficult task of picking up the pieces and recovering from the altered reality you face.

Before the scammer called, your financial situation was stable. It may not have been perfect, but it was where you left it. During the conversation, someone altered your view of your account. Although only a few words were spoken, you accepted their inaccurate vision. From that new perspective, you provided access to your finances. The caller's words and images changed your perception. Once your view was altered, you did what you felt was necessary to protect your funds.

This scenario is not uncommon. Today, we can have more interactions in one day than we encountered in several weeks in the past. The methods of our interactions have changed, and the impact on our wellbeing has escalated. As our encounters increase, the fallout from our transactions weighs heavily on us. Although many of these encounters are short, brief transactions, the impact can be as potent as a long-term relationship. This heightened level of engagement with others exposes us to elevated stress, less emphasis on caring for ourselves, and greater emphasis on material outcomes instead of personal intentions. Your wellness has become a greater individual responsibility because many modern transactions rely on technology rather than face-to-face interactions.

Although the cell phone has become a convenient means of delivering calls, it's one of many ways life interrupts our presence. Any interaction, including conversations, emails, texts, posts, and chats, affects our outlook. We're also surrounded by marketing material and other media calling for our attention. Once our interest is captured, a call can easily influence our thoughts, disturb our mood, and modify our behavior.

When someone attempts to gain your attention it's a call. It's a knock on the door of your awareness. But it's your answers to calls that ultimately alter your life. You don't answer when you accept the call, reply to the email, or respond to a tweet. Instead, you answer through the internal activity occurring during and following the interaction. You begin your answer during the correspondence so it may be difficult to identify, but the greater impact of the call is the opportunity to change your thoughts, views, and even your self-concept through your response.

Our answer to every call depends on how we're touched by the message. We answer by allowing it to mentally and emotionally shift our state of being. We answer by opening our minds, welcoming ideas, and allowing them to move us. Calls are the entry points for the thoughts, images, and emotions we'll find ourselves wrestling with tomorrow. They alter our view of ourselves, others, and the world.

Initial Response

Our response to a call begins when we welcome the message, which ignites a shift. If we accept the idea being presented, it could alter our mindset. That impacts our reasoning, and if appealing or offensive, could change our self-concept. Our responses aren't always vocal or physical at that moment. Sometimes, we hold back and allow our response to remain dormant. One of the most harmful responses to calls is accepting an idea or belief that discreetly alters your thinking. Although it appears that you abandoned the situation, you may be retaining a harmful idea within.

You may not know anything about the caller or their stance. You only know that someone spoke, and you became attentive to their words, or you watched a clip on your media feed that stole your attention. Once we allow a caller to tap into our presence of mind, they can easily influence our thoughts and spark internal conflict or misguided physical reactions. The adverse impact of our response could emerge immediately, but the long-term impact on our awareness could linger undetected.

Altering Your View

During any interaction, a caller can alter your perspective and encourage you to respond. The scam caller attempted to move your view of your finances by inspiring fear and panic. The image he painted caused you to act to prevent a problem that never existed. Our reactions to false narratives can cause us to create actual losses through our responses. Often, we endorse our outcome by allowing callers to change our outlook and opinions, including our self-image.

There's a similar effect when we view disturbing media on social platforms. Although it's normal to run into things we're not comfortable with, how far are we going to let it move us? Are we going to let it push us to speak or act irrationally, or can we release it on demand? Are we going to let it alter our view of ourselves? If we aren't using our awareness, we could invite disharmony without knowing it.

We can also be led astray by an innocent mistake. A colleague discussing a new policy on employee benefits could incite a problem. The policy will have a detrimental effect on your living situation, and you realize that you'll have to make a change. After spending a week stressing over the new rule, complaining to everyone you know, and allowing it to affect your attitude, work performance, and state of mind, you discover the policy will only impact new employees. The inaccurate information you accepted from a trusted source sparked an inner disturbance that changed your outlook. Relying on that false information caused an unnecessary period of stress and anxiety, which affected unrelated areas of your life.

Delivering Demands

We constantly receive calls that place demands on our consciousness. These calls are appeals to invest in something the caller is offering. Investing always includes alternate pathways to move your thoughts and perspective in a new direction. If a caller touches you through fear, anger, flattery, or any emotion they inspire, they've won the opportunity to alter your outlook, mood, and behavior. That increases the chance that you'll wholeheartedly answer their request as they desire. Although we don't recognize it, calls are life's requests, asking us to confirm our current position on everything we face. If we stick with our outlook, our response will show that we're committed to our current view. But, if we react in opposition to what we claim by changing our thoughts and actions, that will prove that we've moved in a different direction. We have to stay alert to observe this tussle occurring within ourselves.

Calls are a part of life's impartial justice system. It demands that we take the witness stand and mentally, physically, and emotionally demonstrate our position on the issues we face. If you've decided to move on from relationships with a particular type of person, life will send someone with those characteristics your way to prove your fidelity. If you've decided to be more patient with others, an annoyance will arrive to challenge your tolerance. If you claim you no longer abuse alcohol, life sends a caller demanding that you prove it. **Your answers to these calls become your life.** But the deeper impact that some calls have will cause internal issues that affect us far beyond the moment.

No Escape

It would be difficult to function without callers in our lives. They spark relationships, inspire social interactions, and are essential to conducting business. But, during these necessary transactions, our minds are open to receiving constructive or detrimental influence. You can quit social media, limit other means of access, or install a "Do Not Disturb" sign on your consciousness, but that won't be enough to transform your life. While it would limit your exposure, you will still have interactions that offer the same opportunities to influence. At the same time, you'll lose the beneficial aspects these outlets offer which enhance our lives.

As much as we may try, we will never have total control over the situations we encounter. If we want to remain engaged in life to experience its positive aspects, we can't hide from the elements we meet. We can't live in fear and avoid the circumstances that approach. That would only increase our stress and anxiety. We have to build assurance within ourselves to control access to our awareness as we step into the world.

Instead of worrying about what callers bring to us, we need to establish ourselves in a state that offers clarity in the midst of any detrimental influence we may face.

That is the desired level of wellness we can obtain. We must empower our outlook and mindset as callers approach and offer their opinions, philosophies, and theories. Then, we'll find ourselves better prepared to deal with the aftermath of their calls.

Control

We can't control what callers offer us from their platforms. We can only manage our presence and awareness. That allows us to balance the influences as they approach. By establishing our presence and elevating our awareness, we can ensure we are fostering wellness. Most callers never reveal the true impact they will have on your life because they don't know how you'll respond. Even if they have an agenda, they're depending on you to allow it to develop. As you're reading this book, I have an agenda for you to become cognizant of calls and their impact. It's up to you to ensure you remain in control by not allowing invalid influences to supply your options instead of creating your own.

We're receiving more calls today from more outlets than at any other point in history. That makes us pioneers that future generations will study to see the effect that this initial era of constant contact had on our lives. We are the test subjects that will show the impact of instant accessibility on our mental and physical wellness. Although that information will be valuable in the future, you need to know the effect in the present. You must determine how this influx is affecting your mindset, attitude, and outlook because it undoubtedly plays a significant role. If you don't know its impact, you can shift your awareness to discover how it's impacting your life.

The Mindful Moment

Chapter 2

How Callers
Take Control

When we receive a call, we may encounter someone with a sincere desire to establish an authentic relationship. Those encounters become assets we should welcome and allow to flourish in our lives. Unfortunately, we also receive many calls that lack favorable qualities. It's easy to recognize the possible negative impact when a caller requests your financial data. It's not so obvious when a caller approaches with kindness and simply asks for your attention. You may not realize that you're exchanging it for a commitment you can't see at that moment. Every time you receive a call, it's a request for access to your awareness. Once accessed, the caller has the opportunity to inspire, discourage, or confuse you.

When callers approach, they use their creativity to bring their vision to life. They may use calculated words, a specific tone, and other colorful presentation methods to usher you into answering their call. They prepare the foundation by arousing your emotions. Your inner voice may question their approach, but your emphasis on animating the words you're hearing, reading, or observing can overpower the internal warning. While looking past that warning, you surrender control by giving the caller access. Instead of realizing you've surrendered your presence of mind, you focus on the new perspective they're selling.

Perspective

This attack on our awareness occurs every moment of our lives. We're constantly creating from someone's vision. If we don't identify the images and voices we're using to make decisions, we'll construct our lives from someone else's imagination instead of creating from our own. That isn't always detrimental because we need guidance, support, and motivation in many situations. We have to open our minds to learn new, valuable information. Others can always offer us genuine support as we're establishing new foundations. But, when we encounter callers whose intentions aren't honorable, we become vulnerable to creating things that don't align with our well-being. We must become familiar with this internal activity because this influence always alters our views.

Simply being exposed to new concepts and ideas doesn't mean we should embrace them. That could create a new home within you. When we surrender subjective control of our mind, we open ourselves to welcoming any image created. Those images offer contrasting views that feed thoughts, emotions, and actions. One perspective could be the inspiration you need to uplift you, while another could be the influence that corrupts your view or depletes your positive self-image.

Facts

Although objective facts are available, subjectivity arrives the moment someone articulates them, and we accept them in that altered form. That leads to the multiple variations that guide and distort our perspectives. Unfortunately, we can't overcome what we embrace until we consciously intervene and change our position. We may try to casually rearrange our thinking, but if we continue to internally accept our current view, we'll continue to experience the results from that perspective.

We always face the possibility of hearing subjectively influenced "facts" when we receive calls. Unfortunately, those facts have been intentionally corrupted to persuade or entice us. When we accept them, they alter our reasoning and understanding. That has a tremendous effect on our awareness and our ability to perceive truth.

There is always discomfort alerting us to question the specifics of what a caller brings, but we often ignore those warnings and accept the images the caller supplies. If we lived in a perfect world, we would easily recognize misinformation and return to a clear outlook. But we live in a world of constant fluctuation and change that doesn't always provide clarity.

We find ourselves facing unpleasant callers in the most innocent situations. They use the same approaches commonly used to spark any relationship. But, when someone understands your vulnerabilities through conversation, observation, or fishing for information, they can befriend you if they're righteous or victimize you if they're insincere. Then, you could find yourself drowning in an unhealthy relationship or unwelcome predicament.

Every experience in a toxic relationship begins with a call. Your unchanging answer to those calls allows the relationship to continue. As you continue to answer the calls with the same response, you're confirming your agreement to accept the inappropriate situation. Although someone else lays the foundation by placing the call, you welcome their desire through your answer. That's when you invite unease, stress, and turmoil. If you aren't managing seemingly innocent situations, your inappropriate responses to calls can manifest as overthinking, anxiety, and depression.

Chapter 3

Stuck

We could never stop life from sending calls. We need to discover creative and productive ways to answer them. A caller may have bad intentions, but you have to cooperate to allow any harm to develop. You have to give away your attention and yield your presence before the call can sprout into adversity. Your response always determines the impact the call will have moving forward. Most of the calls we receive are harmless requests. Some even intend to help us improve our lives. But any call can turn into a disruption when we mishandle our responses.

Every day, we live based on our accepted beliefs and ideas. Those views are the tools we use to construct our world as we answer the calls we receive. Many of our tools are positive and nourishing, while others add to our suffering. We mistakenly invite disharmony into our personal lives, and our collective negligence can harm the world.

As we dwell on our situations, we're also feeding the state of being we've adopted to manage them. If our conditions are favorable, we'll continue to feed off that comfort until another call throws us off. Likewise, if our circumstances are discouraging, we'll continue to feed off that negative state. Feeding off that unproductive state guarantees we'll remain married to it until we accept a call with positive influence.

Traditional teachings used parables and stories that display this effect that exists within our situations. In modern times, we say that the rich get richer, and the poor get poorer. Unfortunately, we automatically think of finances when we consider rich versus poor. But rich and poor identify our condition related to everything we face, not just our financial state.

Beyond the Response

The way you answer calls is often the source of your problems when stuck in a negative pattern. Many of the situations you're facing are the results of your responses. If you were struggling financially, you can't expect to recover from your situation by continuing to repeat your current practices. You know you need to make an adjustment. The same is true for any situation. You have to discover your current practice to determine your faults. Then you make an adjustment.

That adjustment is a change in response to the situations you face. But you have to ensure you observe the results of your adjustments because they may not be fruitful. Sometimes, your responses can even lead to unhealthy habits you develop to help manage the problems. Unfortunately, many of these new habits become obstacles that add to your baggage while also offering the temporary relief you're seeking.

The weight of the world leans upon everyone. We're forced to carry the load we've inherited and add the weight we create for ourselves along the way. As we bear this weight, life's calls continue to approach. Our families, friends, careers, and many other issues merge to produce this weight. We could reject many of the calls we receive, but life doesn't always offer us that option. We have responsibilities and needs that require us to answer the calls. How we answer them always adds to the weight we've gathered, but it can also relieve us of the burdens and the suffering when we use our awareness to remain present during our transactions.

Many of our problems originate when something moves us from our place of comfort (which many of us don't experience often) to a state of unease. Your comfort zone may not be acceptable to others, but it's the place you've accepted as your home. It's your sanctuary. Out of the blue, something comes along and knocks you out of your comfort to deal with life. That becomes the moment of impact. Your mind starts running as if you were a director considering different scenes for a movie. The call can shift your thoughts and displace your stability. It's the moment you abandon your ease to accept disorder, and it always emerges from a call.

You may not recognize this moment because the effect won't be apparent immediately, but this is the moment you surrender control. From this point, you could find yourself making acquaintance with undesirable aspects that appear instead of rejecting them. That discomfort can expand and affect unrelated areas of your life from the new state you invited.

Refusal to Upgrade

You may know someone deeply invested in a toxic relationship that they refuse to leave. It may be difficult to watch them suffer, but you can't make them walk away. They've learned to accept the pain and disappointment they're experiencing. It's become a regular part of their life. For them, that interaction is better than being alone. You can offer your friend everything in the world to convince them to escape their predicament, but you can't release them from their attachment to the relationship. You have to allow them to spiritually detach from it. That's when your help can make a difference. You can't give them what they need to transition out of their current state. That must occur internally.

Like a toxic relationship, you can't elevate from any conditions without upgrading your state of being. You can educate yourself with new information, but that may not be enough to cause you to change your perspective. You'll continue to react from your current state, which will land you in similar predicaments. Ancient spiritual teachings stressed that you look beyond the current difficulty to see the solution. You can respond from a composed space when you downgrade your focus on the negative aspects of the problem.

The situation you face represents the mountain you must overcome. Dwelling on the mountain will spiritually freeze you in a problematic state. That causes you to react in ways that will ensure you remain attached to the problem. You must adjust your state of being during the physical struggle to evolve. We can't continue to answer and dwell within irrelevant calls while we look up at a mountain that won't go away. We have to adjust our answers to every call to ensure we are making the right moves that will lead us in a positive direction.

If we step back and view what's occurring from an immaterial perspective, it could help us see how we remain stuck in cycles. We receive input from the world, which are the calls to our consciousness. We respond to the calls with our reactions. Life accepts our response and reciprocates based on our response. We then receive life's new response and react again. If we continue to respond to life from the same mental and spiritual states, we can expect similar responses from the world. That's how we find ourselves anchored in repeated patterns. Our reactions tell the world who we are and what we believe. We fulfill our purpose in life through the answers we send out through our responses. That's the true foundation of our existence.

This scenario is natural for everything we face in life. It's easier to view our relationships with people, but we have relationships with everything we encounter. We create abstract relationships with ideas, beliefs, and concepts that affect us as intensely as our relationships with people. We can facilitate changes when we begin to see our relationship with the concepts and ideas we encounter so we can move forward with our lives. Inner adjustments aren't a change in thoughts that approach us; they're a change in how we allow things to affect our being. They're a change in perceptions and interactions. Once they change, negative thoughts may approach, but they won't have total control over your emotions and your ability to move forward.

Recycling

We may want to improve our position, but our relationships and conditions can attach us to our scenario. Our struggle to move forward isn't with the world; the conflict is within ourselves. We've become comfortable with the mismanagement of our circumstances, and we continue to answer life's calls from that stance. Although finding comfort in our lives can be essential to enduring difficult times, we must be willing to release that comfort and advance to face new opportunities when they arise. We can manage our comfort by looking outside of the present trouble and attaching to one of the solutions we discover. That occurs spiritually. The current events attach us to the present scenario when we feed off them. When we transcend the present suffering and view our desired state, we can begin to move toward our healing.

Our lives are a string of circumstances that require responses. Each response offers an opportunity to convey our personal beliefs and philosophies to the world. When we apply our paintbrush to the world's canvas through our words and actions, we are fulfilling the purpose of our existence. We're expressing our essence through our physical existence. We're using our lives to bring thoughts, beliefs, and ideas into reality.

When situations occur, we respond from our current state of being. That reaction always triggers a response from the external world. Those replies come from friends, coworkers, family members, authorities, strangers, or whoever we encounter. Their reactions affect the current situation and can alter our mindset moving forward. The way these responses touch us can create an endless loop. That spiritual loop is powerful enough to keep us cemented in our circumstances for a lifetime, or at least until we decide to alter our state of being and responses. But we won't recognize the activity if we aren't using our inner awareness.

This cycle makes it difficult to escape the predicaments we've lived with and have come to accept over time. Our refusal to change our approach, outlook, and attitude is arresting. Although life is moving on, we can't move past our current position. We've refused to change how we answer calls. When our spiritual home is not a fruitful place of existence, it will continue to contribute to our nonproductive or even hostile environment.

Discovering Presence

Before allowing this to continue, we have to rediscover the ease we abandoned before the call. We must find a way to elevate our awareness instead of our old presumptions. We must change how we corrupt our outlook when answering calls to establish a healthy, consistent nature as a foundation. The perspective we're attempting to maintain isn't a physical state or a mindset. The authentic posture we need to obtain comes through our presence.

Practicing presence means you're aware of your current environment, and you're observing your position within it. You're aware that your senses are assessing the conditions, your mind is assigning meaning to your surroundings, and your being is a witness and participant in the activity. As you assign meaning to the environment, you're preparing the foundation that you will use to answer calls. Presence means you're aware of the lens you're using to observe life and understand the perspective you're using to interpret your observations. You remain in control as you receive feedback on your assessment. You're not allowing yourself to judge and react to circumstances haphazardly. You're moving with balance and poise, and that's controlling your demeanor and your reactions.

When we aren't present, our state of being fluctuates with every call we receive. We bounce in and out of moods and attitudes without warning. We're also unable to explain how we create fortunate or unfortunate circumstances because things just seem to happen to us. When we experience organic happiness and success, we won't be able to sustain it because we don't know how we obtained it. We also won't be able to identify what we may have done to invite anger or depression into a situation.

The activities we're facing might be physically or mentally demanding, but presence allows us to move with clarity. It offers confidence to proceed with an unbothered strength. It's the connection between the world we observe and our internal interpretations of what we witness. If we're not actively engaging in presence, the alternative perspective we're using to interpret our surroundings remains in control.

Repressed

When we fail to recognize how our interpretations impact our thoughts and emotions, the weight we experience always grows. The goals we can't reach, the habits we can't eliminate, and the transformations we can't complete are fueled by our inability to embrace presence. Our departure from the present moment blocks us from ever seriously attempting to improve our circumstances. While maintaining our thoughts on our problems, we allow the present to escape. We try to change habits and alter our actions, but we can't overcome the impact of our current outlook anchoring us in our problems. That outlook continues to feed us. Unfortunately, our attempts to advance are in vain until we recognize and address that source.

We believe we would never create discomfort for ourselves, so we don't consider our inner contributions. Instead, we accuse external factors of creating our circumstances because we can always find someone to blame. We might focus on the individuals who upset us or the events we encountered but refuse to adjust our outlook in the present. We won't see ourselves reacting from the same perspective that moved us into the scenario.

Restore

Presence allows us to examine the internal activity brewing in real time. It prevents us from outwardly provoking a situation that needs inner attention, not a hostile response. It gives a broad perspective that can prevent irrational responses. Our awareness is multi-layered, yet we tend to rely on our external observations while subduing our internal activity. The most potent use of awareness occurs when we observe and assess both aspects. Often, we become preoccupied with animating the exterior scene with our words and actions. Without looking within, we'll never determine why we allow some problems and unproductive perspectives to persist.

Our internal activity works involuntarily. It impacts every aspect of our lives. Things you want to make primary in your life are pushed aside so something you have a stronger attachment with can prevail. When we overlook our inner activity, it affects life without our conscious input. When we act without awareness, we might begin to rearrange aspects of our lives inadvertently. We won't recognize the effect of our essence until results physically appear in our lives.

We disregard a vital part of life when we don't consider our presence. As a result, we miss the answer to many of the frustrations we face. Instead of considering our presence, we use other methods to resolve life's problems. Sometimes, we even compromise our ethics and morals to manipulate situations. Our awareness can help us identify that desperation and anxiety early on. It alerts us before we move in a morally or ethically compromising direction. It's the compass that leads us to the natural resolution of life's scenarios. But we must be present to receive and understand these warnings.

Life has given us many responsibilities. None may be more important for our wellness than managing the beliefs and ideas we adopt and sustain. Although we're born under parental protection, we eventually become liable for the beliefs we've accepted. They become the foundation of our awareness and guide our answers to calls.

The Mindful Moment

Chapter 4

The Mindful Moment

There's a crucial moment during every call that leads our response. It occurs before we say, do, or produce anything. It's the moment we reach our understanding of the caller's message and initiate a reaction. Discovering this moment is enlightening because it's the moment we shift from receiving empty words to assigning personal meaning to them. From there, we contemplate our next move and deliver actions. That instant is essential in determining how the call will affect our lives. If we bypass our awareness, we might rely on the feeling aroused by the caller at that moment to dictate our response instead of making an informed choice based on our intentions.

This moment is also heavily targeted by those desiring to trigger us into action, but it lives within our control. Every marketing department, successful influencer, and savvy caller knows this vital point in our transactions. Sadly, it's not a requirement that we discover this moment. In this crucial moment, we could prevent many of the problems we create for ourselves and those we accept from others. But we're free to ignore it and allow it to dictate our lives subconsciously.

Four-Step Response Process

There are four phases we progress through as we answer calls. Identifying your journey through these steps in your responses can stimulate change by revealing details about your mindset, beliefs, and true intentions. Each stage also offers an opportunity to change your direction and take control of your circumstances. These stages are your primary opportunity to direct your life positively.

Phase 1

The first stage begins before receiving the call. Every response begins with our presence. Our temperament, attitude, and disposition at any moment are the primary contributors to our response. That state of being in the moment we receive a call always takes the lead. When the caller approaches, our mindset, emotional state and the setting each play a dynamic role in our response.

Phase 2

The second phase centers on our attention. When we receive the call, we have to determine how much attention we intend to apply to it. We can fully engage, casually address, or indifferently ignore the request for our attention. It might be easy to ignore calls, but we will miss out on the essential requests we need to receive. That means we have to apply some of our attention to the calls we receive in most circumstances. We have to determine if the call is worthy of our attention.

Phase 3

The third phase arrives after we've applied our attention to the call and received the information. In this phase, we make the crucial decision to accept the idea, reject it, or allow it to exist without impact. This decision will go far in mentally and emotionally influencing us moving forward.

Phase 4

Finally, in the fourth phase, we display our response to the call. We allow our internal response to flow to the surface through our reaction. We either acknowledge the call by verbally or physically responding or by turning away and blowing off the request. We assume that this ends the call, but it could be the beginning of an influence that alters our perspective, mindset, mood, or state of being for an undetermined period.

Collateral Damage

Unexpectedly, you may follow up on calls you thought you previously ended. These are the issues we must identify and the primary reason we must become more discerning about the calls we accept. The residual effect of these resurfacing issues and the responses they ignite are a source of the troublesome overthinking that disturbs our presence.

An external observer could study your reactions in life and offer a diagnosis, but that diagnosis is solely based on your observable responses. Only you see what's internally occurring before you act. You can determine if your reactions are pure or if you've internally decided to adjust your response before presenting it to the world. That's the extreme level of intimacy each of us has with life that no one can interrupt without our consent. It's also why counseling can be difficult without the sincere honesty and openness that naturally exists within

The understanding of life we've adopted always takes the lead when we answer calls. That understanding is crucial because it feeds our thoughts and actions. We all have biases from the many influences that formed our outlook. It's our responsibility to identify the unbalanced perspectives we hold that came with those influences. They may mislead us when we assign meaning to what we're experiencing. They also misguide us when responding to life's calls. We can't begin to settle our minds and calm our thoughts until we investigate our perspectives. That will show us where we may be adding anxiety due to our perceptions and misinterpretations.

We won't commit to moving in our desired direction if we're not internally aligned. We may go through the motions that can lead us on the right path, but the alternative aspects life offers and those we're internally committed to will continue to control our actions. We have the option to pursue the countless calls we receive throughout the day or decide to create our own commitments to follow. Learning to seize control of our essence without allowing anyone, any thought, or any situation to redirect our spirit is vital. Without this level of control, our prior routines and habits will continue to dictate our lives because they have a bond cemented over time. We may flirt with alternative ideas that could improve our lives, but the bonds we already own won't lay down and allow us to move away from them.

You rarely complete your answer to a call during the encounter. The interaction may have ended, but the impact on your life may have just begun. That impact may continue for the rest of your life. If you don't control your responses to life's calls by managing your inner awareness, the adverse effects from calls will continue to damage your presence.

The Mindful Moment

Chapter 5

Subconscious Boundaries

We have inner agreements with life that we've set as guides for our thoughts, emotions, and actions. These agreements form subconscious boundaries. We establish these agreements when we initially encounter something or when someone teaches, influences, or advises us. Whenever we face the concept or idea in the future, we reaffirm that initial agreement and proceed within its boundaries. An example of an agreement with life is discovering we're allergic to a substance. When we're exposed to it and experience an allergic reaction, we develop an agreement to avoid it. That sets a rule for our behavior in the future.

We create new guidelines through experiences and lessons we learn as we observe life. Identifying them is essential because we must ensure they aren't limiting or harming us. Recognizing the benefits of an agreement about an allergy is easy, but some of the arrangements we've set aren't beneficial to our mental, physical, or emotional wellness. Mistakenly, we allow them to persist without investigating their origins and determining how they may negatively impact us.

Our agreements also establish the amount of an emotion or feeling we're willing to accept from the calls we receive. As we approach the boundary of an agreement, we're forced to respond. Sometimes, we respond with verbal or physical outbursts. In other circumstances, we uncomfortably welcome the feeling and allow it to disturb our presence. If we understand our agreements and realize we're reaching our limit, we can learn to confront our discomfort early instead of allowing the situation to control us.

Jurisdiction

These internal mandates are far more binding than any formal contracts we've signed because they don't need a judge to enforce them. They are self-executed. There isn't a committee ensuring our agreements are valid. Yet, we rely on them to guide our lives. We set the boundaries for everything we will accept through these agreements. They overrule the plans we make and reject the goals we set that attempt to oppose their control. Our agreements even outsmart the applications we install on our cell phones and devices that help us manage our lives. They cause us to press the snooze or ignore button or delete the app we downloaded to help us.

These agreements align us with our true beliefs about life and our position. They ensure our actions remain consistent with the understanding we've established for ourselves and maintaining our status in life's hierarchies. These underlying covenants tie us to our innermost intentions and lead our answers to calls. They also guide us to bypass commitments to ideas and concepts that don't align with our agreements, even if the idea could improve our well-being. They impact every area of our lives by forming the framework for our thoughts and actions. If we ever consider how we're genuinely moving our world, we'll see that we typically stay within the boundaries of our agreements. Unfortunately, we don't recognize that a random event, unfortunate situation, or a biased mentor could be the source of an agreement.

Preoccupied

Many of us aren't aware of our current agreements with life. We know what we're physically doing every day, but we may not be completely aware of the source of our thoughts, words, and actions or their internal impact. Instead, we go from day to day in line with our agreements, many of which have become subconscious. Then, when we set goals or desire to move into a better position, we become frustrated with our struggle because we can't pinpoint the internal source of opposition.

Ambitious, determined, and focused people align their agreements with their true intentions. When opportunities that challenge their agreements approach, they recognize them and react. When calls arrive that will create separation from their intentions, they don't embrace them. From the outside, everything they do perfectly aligns, but that isn't the case. When they receive a call that isn't in sync with their agreements and mistakenly accept it, they don't let the situation continue to damage their intentions. When they recognize the misalignment, they find the opportunity to alter their answer to the call to ensure they realign with their agreements. They don't allow the misalignment to drive them further away, regardless of how long they spend answering ill-advised calls. They don't surrender and accept the new direction these distractions offer.

This determination to align with your agreements sounds fantastic, but that focused connection can also be detrimental. When our agreements are leading us to destructive ends, the ambitious link still powerfully connects you to it. In this case, instead of an attraction to something positive, we may increase our connection to something negatively impacting us. We can maintain the same loyalty to a negative agreement as we have with a positive one.

We all own agreements we align with that we don't recognize, yet they exist. There are situations you've experienced, both positive and negative, that seemed to play out without your input. But if you look back, you may find that you had an underlying agreement that led you to your outcome. When calls arrived that you knew you shouldn't have answered, you accepted them without hesitancy. Those replies helped place you someplace you didn't intend to go.

Participating

We feel like things arbitrarily happen because we don't see ourselves aligning with the result in the moments that we act. But, as we're answering the calls we receive, our responses place us exactly where our answers lead us. If we're not going in the direction we believe we should, we have to inventory our agreements. We likely have a hidden arrangement that's leading us to our current situation.

Many of our actions may seem habitual, but we have margins that we align within. These are the guides that we've set as our boundaries. We must identify and become familiar with them because they are the agreements controlling our lives. Unknowingly, we may have given personal power to people and ideas around us because we haven't been managing our inner agreements.

Although our self-identities come from our concepts of ourselves, our identities don't originate from within. For most of us, it comes from the influences that have educated, mis-educated, or otherwise influenced us concerning who we are. That influence continues daily, and much of it may not be best for our well-being. We have choices in every situation we face, but our self-concept and agreements can predetermine our options.

Sadly, in some cases, there are options that we won't even consider for ourselves because of our self-concept and the agreements we've aligned with to conduct our lives.

It can also be easier to accept that someone else has power or control over us than to admit that we have mandates within ourselves, causing us to sustain our bad habits and behaviors. We may be allowing someone else to control us because we aren't willing to take on the responsibility of managing our lives. With practice and a new understanding, we can confront our agreements and recover that power and control we may have inadvertently surrendered.

Chapter 6

Outdated Agreements

Our internal agreements aren't necessarily facts, yet we allow them to control our outlook. Many of our agreements may have been appropriate earlier in our lives but are no longer relevant as they've become outdated. That's why we must identify them and address those that may be harmful because they significantly affect our presence. Our agreements were influenced by biased humans (we all have biases), with limited outlooks (we haven't seen everything), and incomplete sciences (human knowledge grows as we advance). We could be relying on faulty perspectives supported by flawed agreements.

Many things are beyond our control, but our responses are a chance to contribute to the scenario. Although various reactions are available, we reach into our established agreements to form our reactions. Our responses to these uncontrolled scenarios harmonize with our agreements unless we allow the situation to determine our response. When that happens, we surrender our chance to improve the situation and allow the caller to control our response.

When the weight of the world shows up, it disturbs our presence and derails our commitment to our goals, but our allegiance to our inner agreements and habits remains intact. We become so preoccupied with the weight approaching that we don't recognize when our agreements negatively alter new goals and intentions. Our obsession with external issues distracts us, causing us to suffer and surrender our dreams in frustration.

Imposing

Our goals are actually rivals to the agreements we currently own. If we were already in agreement with the focus of our goal, it wouldn't be a target we're striving toward. It would already be an agreement we have, not something we're trying to obtain. A goal is an attempt to change the inner contracts that don't align with what we want to achieve or experience. You can succeed at your goal when you establish a new agreement that's immovable by callers and distractions.

We must be careful not to confuse our agreements with life with the casual deals we negotiate within ourselves. When we arrange our agreements with life, consciously or not, we set the boundaries for what we want to give and what we want to accept from life. That establishes the basic guidelines for our actions. Conversely, when we set agreements with ourselves, we are more flexible. We allow ourselves to divert from the intent of these arrangements freely. That freedom allows us to change those agreements, but that also makes them easy to tune out when they could be something we need to adhere to. They include the goals and desires we establish but are challenging to obtain. An example is our attempts to stop bad habits. We may desire to stop, but it's not pressing.

When we treat goals as simple agreements, we don't give them priority. That's important because our struggles to adhere to our desired outcomes impact our presence and how we see ourselves behind closed doors. The deals we make on the surface must align with our deeply rooted agreements if we want them to develop. When they don't, they'll continue to impact our presence negatively.

If there's a position you want to obtain, it becomes a goal; if there's a task you want to accomplish, it's a goal; even the type of person you desire to become is a goal. In every case, we set goals to advance through the stages we need to progress. If there are aspects of our goals that conflict with our agreements with life, we'll face difficulty. Unfortunately, we may not discover the foundation of our trouble if we aren't familiar with our underlying agreements. We might believe we are fully engaged in achieving our goal, but we have internal resistance. In our confusion, we'll provide logical explanations to justify our struggles. We might believe that we didn't have enough time or that the circumstances were wrong. But we're simply staying aligned with what we've already established with life.

Absolute

When you establish an arrangement with yourself, you may fail to live up to your standard through your actions. When you set an agreement with life, you won't waver when circumstances approach. That's where change must occur. There's a decisive difference between the two. A sincere assessment allows you to differentiate between these similar but distinctly different conditions. You must conduct an internal inquiry to understand your agreements and discover where you stand. This query is crucial and will clarify any confusion you're facing. You may find that your actions align with your true inner agreements.

We face a dilemma when life hands us less than we expected to receive. When life asks more from us than we're willing to give, we also face a problem. How we alter our approach in these situations is crucial because it will determine if we'll establish a new agreement with life or make a simple arrangement with ourselves. These surface agreements that conflict with our agreements with life are destined to cause internal hardship. Much of the overthinking and mind clutter that initiate negative spirals are fed by these non-binding agreements we set within ourselves.

Even though these arrangements don't box us into corners, they establish internal guidelines we attempt to impose on ourselves. The fact that our agreements may not be accurate is irrelevant; the impact on our being remains highly relevant. The adverse effects of our inner conversations show in how we feel about ourselves and how we think others view us. That can surface in how we carry ourselves in the world and definitely affects how we answer calls. We can find ourselves acting out of fear, unnecessarily avoiding things, or fading away into feelings of hopelessness. We won't detect this activity without the awareness to see the suffering we cause ourselves through our agreements. We'll try to cope with our circumstances while our agreements cause unnecessary suffering. True mindfulness tasks us to inventory and understand all of our inner agreements.

The Mindful Moment

Chapter 7

One Essential App

Our inner agreements are essential in controlling our lives. We won't mentally, physically, or emotionally answer calls favorably if we don't recognize our agreements with life. Instead, we'll allow ourselves to move by the external conditions we're already experiencing, which prevents progress.

Fortunately, an app is available to help us understand everything we observe. It's powered by what we know, perceive, and believe in the moment. That app is our awareness. It displays our inner agreements' influence as we assign meaning to what we're witnessing. When using this app, we must be self-aware to increase its reliability and performance.

External events cause us to stray from our preferred actions. But our feelings, moods, attitudes, and beliefs command our impact and direction concerning those events. Knowing this, we should be more concerned with our inner approach as we function within our surroundings.

Our awareness is the only "app" available that alerts us to our status concerning our agreements. As we approach situations, our awareness can identify the specific agreements we are aligning with. No one can force you to move into your desired state of existence. Others can watch your actions and behavior to encourage or criticize you, but the truth lives internally and will eventually prevail. You must agree to commit with your inner being and not simply with words. That's your aim, and you fail by remaining attached to the old agreements.

Inner Influence

Your state of being can impact your circumstances more than your actual encounters with the people and things you deal with. Your approach can cause a negative situation to develop before the encounter ever has a chance to be fruitful. On the other hand, it can create a manageable environment in an otherwise intolerable situation. Awareness lets you approach life with the proper mindset without sparking unnecessary problems.

When you decide to alter your conditions and attempt a transformation, you must realize that internal changes might not occur overnight. But they can occur over time. So, while transitioning, understand that the next week, month, or year can reveal the person you want to be if you persist with your renewed agreements. However, if you remain attached to your old agreements, you can expect next week to stay the same as this week.

When you tune out your agreements with life, you've decided to travel anywhere the wind blows. You'll continue to act on impulse and allow personally uninspired or externally influenced views to run your life.

You can seek guidance through counseling and other types of mentoring to gain understanding, but the responsibility to know yourself can't be passed on to anyone else. Others can help you, but you can't escape your primary role. Others can help you discover factors that cause your attitudes, mood swings, and ill-advised habits and behaviors, but they can't internally direct you. So, you have to do the work.

Unfortunately, some people will try to take the responsibility of controlling your life away from you. They'll find ways to use you for their purpose. Life is precious. If you don't move in your preferred direction, someone else may attempt to control you. They'll use you to advance their agendas and move them closer to their goals. You can spend your entire life serving them, working for them, being entertained by them, buying their products, and supporting them in other ways.

You may be satisfied with your situation and continue reaffirming your internal agreements. If not, you must decide to take on the responsibility of choosing a different direction. Then, you can create an agreement to move in that direction. But, even when you find comfort, life can interrupt it with various disruptions. Awareness can help you retain that comfort when your issues offer instability.

You have energy within you that you can use to improve yourself, or you may choose to give it away, allowing others to use it. The choice is yours. Just remember that you solidify your circumstances by affirming them every day. Again, it's always easier to reaffirm your current arrangement than to construct a new one. You need to internally prepare for change if you want it to become your reality.

Retaining Control

Our awareness provides the balance we need to navigate life. It helps us accomplish our worldly requirements and develop maturity. It might feel like we don't have much input in some of our experiences, but we must acknowledge our impact on our lives. That allows us to use that impact to our benefit instead of allowing it to damage our situations further. We may not be able to change some things that touch our lives, but we can respond in ways that reduce the effect.

If we fail to develop a relationship with our awareness, we become the greatest enemy of the challenging issues we face. We'll continue to misinterpret our experiences as the end instead of the means to wisdom and understanding. We'll exist as the enemy to ourselves instead of becoming the partners with life we should be. We'll automatically jump to analytical solutions to our problems. Although they may be technically accurate, they don't always reveal what initially led to the problem. Those sources are always found within.

We allow circumstances to move us and never let our unbiased awareness have a stake in our responses. That could be a reason behind some of our suffering, but it is typically overlooked. Abandoning our comfort and moving to a new state stimulated by the latest crisis is a choice. It might go unnoticed, but it has a massive impact on our lives. It's where we filter out all the possible reactions we could have until we reach the one our inner guidance has agreed to manifest. That movement becomes the source of our discomfort or our ease. The difference lies in the influences that are directing us.

The world won't pause for us to recognize this influence. We have to discover this effect amid the circumstances we face. Our awareness will show us how we lead ourselves to the suffering or satisfaction we encounter. Awareness doesn't choose our paths for us; it only helps reveal additional options you may not see when you develop a conscious relationship with it.

When our problems show up, they appear to come from the people and the incidents we encounter. In reality, those interactions are only momentary. Our internal reactions to these encounters create the foundation for our state of being. That effect can last a lifetime, or we can eliminate it as soon as we recognize it. Discovering the aspects that are internally moving you is vital. The sooner, the better.

Identifying the attachments we cling to, which help sustain our discomfort, is also essential. They're also aspects that move us internally. We may not consciously acknowledge their presence, but they affect our disposition. They include the views we've accepted, the knowledge we've accumulated and won't challenge, and the beliefs we passionately hold. A thorough inventory of your attachments and agreements with life will offer clarity throughout life.

Sometimes, we assume our responses are reasonable because they reflect what's widely accepted in society. But why are so many of us struggling with issues that we know are detrimental to our well-being? Why do we find it so difficult to remove ourselves from destructive habits? Many things society considers normal aren't always best for you or society. The journey to wellness is within our sphere of influence but isn't easy to embrace. We must overcome the unreliable agreements we've established to increase our well-being. The power to progress lies within, but the decision to consciously use this power must be accepted and nourished. It's available when we're determined to eliminate ourselves as our enemy.

We quickly uncover the measurable aspects of our interactions; awareness recognizes those that aren't easily observed. Though immeasurable, they affect us as powerfully as the physical elements. We have the opportunity to take any view on the things we encounter. We must consider our internal perspectives instead of letting generic perspectives dominate. We might find that our untainted views don't align with the outlook we've been holding. When you view the world from within, you obtain a fresh, unpolluted perspective that can inspire positive changes in thoughts and actions.

We should try to observe our outlook and feelings toward our situations before we move into action. Watching our overall approach to life can be a start, but we can also look at tiny interactions. Is panic, fear, or anxiety dominating your presence? Are you always preparing for the worst and planning for undesirable circumstances that may never develop? The feelings that overwhelm your presence create your spiritual home and guide your actions. You're leading yourself toward a predetermined destination. Your fear urges you to move with limitations, and anxiety won't allow you to move at all.

There are many definitions of spirituality. One that you must learn to identify with is your nature or essence in the present tense. It is the power behind your actions. Though you have positive and negative qualities and attributes, the ones dominating your overall mood govern your activities. Those traits may not lead you to a comfortable or happy place, but they lead you to your current home. It's the state you're creating from, favorably or adversely. It doesn't have to be permanent, but it's home until you change it or something comes along and causes you to change it.

No one wants to live in constant fear or panic, yet many of us do every day. We also own prejudices and biases that we weren't born with that limit our pure enjoyment of life experiences. We allow some of these fears and biases to rise to the surface and inflict harm on ourselves and others. Often, we don't even realize the damage we're introducing to the world because it isn't our intent. But we must become determined to identify things that are guiding our lives. These disturbances cause destruction in the world, but they also cause turbulence within. You can never enjoy the peace that life offers when stuck in fear or disdain for something. You focus on identifying the aspects you've learned to fear or despise. That causes discomfort that can't be relieved until you recognize and release that contempt.

Our demeanor and attitude will always affect our encounters the way they always have until our spiritual input changes. That feeling or mood that exists within has a dynamic effect on the way we interact with anything we face. That alters the results we'll obtain when the interactions occur.

Life can be one distraction after another. If we allow ourselves to become absent, we'll find it difficult to achieve anything. Our answers to calls will remain unchanged. We'll find ourselves in a constant state of dreaming of success instead of a state of performing. On the other hand, distractions can also help remove our attention from the undesirable conditions we face. We must ensure that the distraction is uplifting us and not freezing us in an unpleasant state. That's the difference between those who perform the steps to their objectives and those who continue to dream. Healthy distractions help us manage our lives, while others keep us tied to unproductive conditions. We can't move forward if we continue to return to our undesired state and settle.

Life approaches us uniquely, and we won't follow the same steps even with the same goals. The route to success will never be the same for two people. The requirements may be the same, but we move in and out of states of being as we complete the steps. Our responses to the calls we receive will determine our progress. It also determines how fast we'll achieve the goal. Those who can balance life and distractions while remaining present will achieve success. Even if that success is the wisdom they gained through failing to achieve the goal.

When we don't know how things affect us, daily events and occurrences constantly disturb our lives. We can find ourselves caught up in the activities of the world while we toss our lives to the side as unimportant. No one can rescue us from that place of nonexistence. We must save ourselves. Experts may counsel us, and friends may try to assist us, but no one can bring your life to the forefront. We must consciously make our existence a priority in the world. Regardless of what anyone has told you that you are.

When we find ourselves in negative states, such as anger and disappointment, we must address them early because they can have an underlying spiritual impact. When we allow them to linger, things can quickly become detrimental. They move us away from uplifting ourselves and leave us dwelling on the negative aspects that arise. Recognizing this activity within is vital. Without awareness, you may drift within the static and confusion of the world without realizing what you're allowing. Discovering and guiding your essence is a crucial step in your maturity.

Spiritual discipline is one of the most important forms of self-control. Establishing control of your state of being doesn't require any external assistance. We own this ability but may not be committed to discovering and applying it. We often allow our state of being to fluctuate instead of harnessing it so it can become an asset. Instead of allowing things to arouse and confuse us, we have the power to maintain our desired state of mind. Life offers unlimited opportunities to move in our chosen direction. We must prove loyalty to our intentions by retaining the essence leading us to our desire. We must confront the subconscious activity we allow to dominate us. We must spiritually align with a state of being we approve of rather than subconsciously falling into an unfortunate one.

Moving without awareness can cause us to view things inappropriately before we experience any insult, disrespect, or offense. We'll mislabel and misinterpret situations if we lead with a biased perspective. We'll view a minor disturbance that offers an opportunity for growth as a personal attack. That incident can spark a negative feeling that blossoms into a hateful or destructive stance, which may impact us for the rest of our lives. Although these encounters could inspire progress, our misinterpretation can allow these events to erupt into major problems in our personal lives. We may struggle in scenarios that appear to be earth-shattering, but many are only opportunities for discovery about ourselves.

We might plant seeds of destruction if we don't see the growth opportunities behind our encounters. We may never overcome that opportunity for growth that we turned into a breeding ground for fear or hatred. When we continue to deny these opportunities in our daily lives, we create doorways to destructive thoughts and actions. Once we open that door, we may cling to an attachment that will be difficult to dissolve.

Our internal attachments are powerful. They compel us to achieve our goals or stop us from accomplishing anything. They can cause us to react reasonably or lead us to move obstructively. Many of our inappropriate actions are rooted in attachments. Inner awareness allows us to respect what we see and hear without spiritually attaching to questionable aspects. It allows us to manage any adverse feelings or emotions we may be attaching to our presence. Like everything in life, we have to actively use our awareness to sharpen it. It can become our primary resource to assist us as we answer the calls life sends.

The Mindful Moment

Part Two

Insufficient Coverage

Chapter 8

Something to
Believe In

It's rare to find time throughout the day that we aren't facing some form of persuasion. Everything we encounter offers influence, but most don't support our best interests. When we're introduced to a new idea, a decision confronts us. We have to determine what we intend to do with it. The pressure to accept it occurs at the critical moment we decide to fully accept the influence, partially accept aspects of it, or totally reject it. Although this process is simple and requires little effort, it dramatically impacts our mindset.

One of the problems when accepting a call is the false belief that you're only validating what appears on the surface. With every call, there are always secondary elements attached. These factors inherently accompany the intended message, but sometimes, that association is intentional. You could read an article with evidence-based facts, but within those facts, you'll find elements designed to influence your view. That is the overwhelming reality that confronts everyone. That can help explain some of the troubling issues in our lives. We may be supporting ideas with unjust aspects attached that we aren't aware of. When we finally see the big picture, we may be deeply invested in a relationship or tied to a negative concept.

Gaining Consent

Persuasion relies on igniting a feeling. Although we should be concentrating on the message, we allow the caller to control our focus. The actual message can become secondary to the caller's ability to touch an emotion. Callers use different techniques to secure that emotional approval through their approach. The strength or comfort in their voice, the beauty or familiarity of the face, the charm or humor they deliver, and many other emotionally deceptive tactics are used to move your emotions. That encourages you to trust the messenger and welcome the message. When you embrace these designed distractions, you allow influencers to manipulate you without objectively earning your acceptance. They've charmed you with deception and disingenuous presentations. You have to disregard these delivery methods during calls.

With this reality of intentional and unintentional influence, we have to realize that the world we must overcome isn't the physical world we encounter. The world that we must overcome is our understanding of the world we've established within. Unfortunately, our perspective may be severely damaged and we're unable to recognize truth due to external tampering and our internal interpretations. Although we can alter our outlook at any moment, we remain tied to the view that we've allowed to exist. We may need help realigning.

Before we can even attempt to alter or release anything, we must acknowledge the amount of influence that exists and the power within it. Even influences that promote positivity emphasize one perspective. You have to search to discover all the unseen aspects because they're the ones that will affect your life.

Making a Connection

It's always important to consider the hidden effects because many influencers aren't interested in sharing the total picture. Their concern is to spiritually move you in the present, not the impact that occurs down the line. Your health and wellness might not be highly considered, especially when there's financial profit to gain.

We're naturally looking for aspects to cling to around the clock. When we consider the amount of influence that targets us, we should admit that our view of the world may contain flaws from manipulated input that we've approved. Our beliefs suffer, and the actions we take that are rooted in flawed influence disturbs our lives. Although we desire and hope for many things, we fight to connect with our beliefs. These are the objects and experiences that we honestly assume we can obtain. We look forward to engaging them even when they're uncomfortable because we have faith in them. Unfortunately, our other desires are only fantasies because we don't honestly believe we can obtain them. That may not be easy to admit, but it's essential to understand. We must use our awareness to discover our actual inner activities.

Our connection to our sincere desire overlooks everything else to ensure it makes the connection. You won't allow anything to disrupt your link to the things you spiritually bond with. You'll go the extra mile to make the connection even when you have to surpass your normal activities. You have to identify these bonds because many exist without your awareness. They may be causing stress and frustration in your life.

We're offered ideas and opinions when we're taught, coached, and entertained. Anything that gains our attention can guide our actions. These ideas influence and manipulate our attitudes and feelings about the subject when we accept them. We assume we're using logic to make the decisions that alter our behavior, but we should look closer. Our reasoning invites us to consider many things, but we don't automatically act based strictly on analysis. We act on the things that spiritually move us and align with our beliefs. Although our logic plays a role, it may not be our primary mover. That distinction may belong to things that touch our subconscious. When our anger moves us to say or do something inappropriate or harmful, haven't we already bypassed reasoning? We've been spiritually moved to action.

When you're feeling pressure to accept a call, you must remain present to consider the total impact of embracing it. We always have options. Although beneficial actions toward our goal are always available, we often act based on our most potent attraction. Unfortunately, that choice may not be in line with your objective. That's a sign that we may at least partially direct our lives with something more powerful than logic.

Amplifying Voices

When something touches you, it affects you emotionally. That puts you in danger of allowing one event to affect other situations that aren't related. A negative influence that touches you can quickly show itself in other areas. It also allows something positive to uplift areas that need encouragement. When we understand the turbulence we experience and how it shows up in our answers to calls, we can learn to address it to enhance rather than disrupt our lives.

If you've never been introduced to your power to control the internal voice that guides you, you won't know how to silence the imposing voices around you.

You won't understand that external voices can't move you; your acceptance of their authority amplifies the volume within you. These voices don't have to speak to you directly. They call your awareness through popular images and concepts. Many of us don't know this because we've silenced our voices and accepted every call since we were toddlers. We haven't learned to appreciate other people's talents and abilities without lowering our value. We've learned to glorify things that others promote while inadvertently devaluing ourselves.

We may be internally hearing how great we are or how extraordinary life is, but many of us listen to voices stating the opposite. These voices may come from familiar faces, but some of the loudest voices come from distant callers and unwritten expectations. In many circumstances, if we don't fit within the boundaries of a particular image, we can feel inadequate. Sometimes, we allow our voices to be silenced by external voices that always help us identify our flaws, fears, and desires. That voice speaks through images and messages on social media, entertainment, advertisements, and other outlets we've allowed to define the human experience.

You can hear life's influences at any volume you choose, but no one can force you to accept and believe it. You can become overly critical of yourself when you compare your situation to the images you're provided. Unfortunately, you may be comparing yourself to staged and unrealistic images. Evaluating yourself can be healthy and beneficial in the right spirit, but your analysis can be hazardous when irrational. You could find yourself subscribing to the ill-advised scrutiny and comments you receive from external sources.

Before deciding what to do with feedback, you must determine if it's being offered in a healthy, impartial spirit. If it's coming from social media and its fabricated imagery, it must be disregarded. That may be hard to do because society has crowned social media and other entertainment sources as the supreme authority of all voices. But we can't allow superficial aspects of society to influence our inner voice because it's rarely beneficial. It doesn't matter what others say or imply about you through words, images, or implications. What you're constantly telling yourself is what you're using to answer life's calls, positively or negatively.

Revisions

When we answer calls inappropriately, our responses may complicate the situation for ourselves and hurt others. When we know we've made a mess, we have to resolve the problem as soon as possible to reduce the impact. We can't allow our mistakes to become our legacy by allowing our pride and ego to take control. Your mistake will leave an impression on the receiver and could invite a negative self-image. You need to address both issues before you move forward.

Some people find themselves in awful situations from their answers to life but won't let those circumstances overpower their presence. They own up to their indiscretion, seek forgiveness, eliminate that response from their database, and abandon the state of being that hosted it. Regardless of any voices of ridicule, they positively transition through their situation to acquire the wisdom it offers. They don't allow others to prevent their growth.

That's a vital part of changing how we answer calls moving forward. The voice that dominates their being is their awareness, which they can control. They don't allow anyone's judgment to tarnish their self-image or outlook on life. They don't let their missteps corrupt the present or predict their future. They move on from the criticism, humiliation, and guilt that attack their spirit and prevent growth.

You must ensure you don't allow mistakes to overpower your spirit. Today always provides a new opportunity to evolve. You must ensure that your internal voice produces an optimistic outlook because you'll answer life's calls with that presence. You'll live in that uninspired state if you settle into a critical image from your miscues. You'll risk falling into a pattern. Unfortunately, repeating these cycles will lower you deeper into distressing scenarios.

You may not be able to escape a negative cycle immediately, but recognizing it gives you a chance to modify your input. Then, you can work on changing your responses. The most significant change is to start monitoring your awareness, which guides your answers to calls. Internal adjustments are crucial to emerging from negative states. The voices you're listening to play a dynamic role in your wellness. You'll surrender to uncertainty if you refuse to control the external voices impacting your life. You have the right to accept direction from others, but their guidance could be inappropriate for your growth.

The sources of the issues that make up the weight in our lives are rarely physical. The impact may arrive physically, but the force that produces the weight may be hidden as it attacks our spirit. The weight comes through our interpretation and the response it stimulates. That creates much of the suffering we experience and alters our state of being. Artificial Intelligence, social media, and any other format depend on our acceptance of an illusion to become a misinformation multiplier. If we don't embrace the negative influences that external sources offer, they can't alter our presence.

Running Away

While we must remain present when answering calls, we must understand that we can't resolve issues by avoiding them. That only applies a bandage, hoping it will naturally repair itself. That's a temporary delay that will eventually lead you back to trouble. You can run from everything but can't hide from the issue behind your problem because it won't subside when you resolve the situation. The issue you have with that specific problem still exists within you.

Perhaps you're considering a new career opportunity because you can't get along with the people you currently work with. You may find temporary relief at the new job, but when you move past the warmth of the introductory phase, your old issues will return. You'll eventually face the same problems without an inner change at your new job. Physical adjustments are only effective when spiritual changes accompany them.

We attempt to fix problems by making physical adjustments or running away. Many times, that only offers temporary relief. The lasting relief we seek is a solution that impacts the soul. You can't resolve inner issues with physical solutions, but we continue to try. We live and breathe in a material world, yet we have an internal presence that affects everything.

We'll discover a new approach when we recognize the activity influencing life outside of our actions. This awareness reveals the multitude of ways we impact life. Unfortunately, most of us never investigate our inner approach to interactions. Instead, we go with the flow and let the things that happen control our movements. But, at some point, we must question our input on our circumstances.

We need to see that our interactions are influenced by more than just the situations we face. We must acknowledge that our essence guides our words and actions as we answer calls. Unfortunately, many of us refuse to question our approaches to situations and relationships to determine if we're comfortable with the circumstances our perspective is leading us toward.

You may know someone who made it through a difficult period in their life. You notice their recovery through the upgraded material possessions in their life. They may have purchased a new car or a bigger house, increased their salary, or achieved another elevated status. But your emphasis on the physical aspects discounts the spiritual transition they endured. As we experience the ups and downs of life from the calls we receive, it's normal to focus on the physical activities occurring. We can easily recall physical aspects; the valuable part we fail to relate to is our emotional state during these stages. We should be more impressed with the inner transformations. We can't alter our circumstances without an internal change away from the former state. The uplifted spirit allows us to visualize something greater. From there, we can creatively move on.

Sometimes, you become angered when a loved one does something disappointing. They may have emotionally wounded you in the process. But the spiritual effect within will outlive your pain, anger, and memory of the event.

Recognizing life's nonphysical impact provides an understanding of the feelings and emotions that seemingly reappear from nowhere. If you aren't aware of what life offers you, you'll continue applying material solutions to immaterial issues. Life presents problems that must be addressed internally first. When we skip this initial step, the concerns linger, disrupting our lives behind the scenes. Every situation has an internal component that discreetly alters our spirit.

Chapter 9

Notifications & Reminders

We're born free to choose the ideas, images, and concepts we want to focus on. Those concepts gain dominion over our thoughts and actions. If we're not honoring our true intentions as we answer calls, we'll welcome conflicting ideas. Everything we let penetrate our minds has the power to influence our behavior. Regardless of our intentions, influences can divert our plans.

Controlling your attention is one of the most significant challenges of life. If you can manage it, all things become possible. Without it, your goals and desires remain possibilities in the distance. If you're unable to direct your attention, you'll never become fully present. You'll continue to chase the unlimited ideas that cross your path.

Directing our attention is an inner process that we overlook, even though it's a key component in controlling our lives. We exchange our presence for entertainment, information, education, and every other aspect we accept. Our ability to choose our point of focus is a form of energy that transforms life through our actions. The primary target of the influence we receive is financial, but money isn't the only valuable asset.

Persuasion begins with a call we accept and allow to withdraw our presence. It ends with a deposit somewhere else that may be permanent. That's the transfer of the idea that confronted our attention, but the change occurring within has a more meaningful consequence. When we view life from its effect on our presence, we'll begin to see the internal repercussions of the influence we receive. The force is unseen but powerful because it alters our feelings, emotions, and actions.

Posted and Informed

It doesn't take much to throw you off your desired path in life. Your attraction to the smallest detail could lead you down an undesirable trail. You immediately begin to lose traction once you're triggered away from your intention. Therefore, when you want to achieve goals, you must be aware of what you're investing in when allowing new interests into your world.

Every day, the media oversaturates us with updated information. You have a choice when you allow this information to enter your mind. You can accept and digest it or let it be entertaining. It truly is that simple. You're relinquishing the power given to you when receiving influence without your conscious consent.

The world may view you as uninformed if you haven't accepted the latest information. That's okay. The problem with investing in this new content is the limited return on that investment. You allow yourself to be intellectually, emotionally, and psychologically affected. Once you buy into it, it isn't easy to release that investment. You can rest assured that the outlets that initially fed you are ready to continue providing you with more.

When we accept what commentators, entertainers, and politicians offer from their platforms, their voices have the potential to misguide us. They have influential professional careers and use their platforms to remain relevant. They have the right to have opinions just as you do, but society gives extra credibility to their views, although unrelated to their success. That's unfortunate because they may create adversity simply for the shock and entertainment value. Their opinion isn't more vital than yours, but they have a platform that supports their views. We must learn to hear their voices as peers and not as authorities.

They've devoted their lives to their craft and the most influential rise to the top. The power they own is their ability to influence others. If they couldn't move people, they wouldn't have found success in their craft. They need others to accept them to be successful. When we individually welcome them, we become the platform that supports their voices. That's how we surrender our power to others. They don't need everyone to support them. The more they gather, the louder their voices and influence become.

Celebrities possess a far-reaching influence on society. Surprisingly, many receive more income from endorsement deals and branding than for their primary work. That demonstrates the importance of persuasion in our world. Some celebrities can't live normally because of our obsession with them. We shouldn't allow familiar faces to dominate our awareness.

Detained in Details

We criticize media outlets for presenting misleading information when they aren't entirely at fault. Instead, we should blame ourselves for investing in things not established in truth. If you weren't a witness, you don't know if the information is accurate, so why would you invest in it? Even if the notification is valid, what does it have to do with your world personally?

Much of what any public figure does is for attention. That doesn't end when the cameras stop rolling. Every time their name is mentioned, their bank account is affected. The bottom line is that the public figure is not at fault. The media outlet that sends out information also isn't to blame regarding your spirit. You cheat yourself when you invest in anything that doesn't provide a valuable return.

The beauty is recognizing that true or false activities don't require your investment. You can allow yourself to be informed about world events without investing. You only need to validate things that promote your wellness and remain unaffected by things that don't.

Social media and other forms of entertainment can be dangerous when we allow them to affect our spirit. We must learn how to keep them in their box and not allow them to impact us personally. We know they influence us to create profit, so we can't become spiritually victimized by them. We shouldn't invest in them improperly, so they begin to affect our being. We have to resist any emotional investing. That's when they move from simple entertainment to becoming negative influences in our world.

Reception

Different forms of entertainment can harm some people while being a positive release for others. You may not need to limit it, but you must know how to answer the calls so they don't impact your presence. The entertainment industry has considerable influence on our culture. Therefore, it must be acknowledged for its impact on your spirit. We need to understand how everything is affecting us spiritually. Things can inspire, motivate, and encourage us but can also disrupt and create overthinking. We must control entertainment's influence on our state of being.

Writers know how to draw attention to attract an audience. The more drama involved in situations, the more enticing they become. That creates big profits for them but can create problems for your state of being. These creators understand human behavior. They know how to include aspects that grab and influence us in ways that may not be healthy. Don't blame the writers, producers, and actors. Our awareness is the key to limiting the effect entertainment has on our presence.

Watching television may be considered a harmful distraction, but the scenarios on the screen aren't much different from what we witness in life. We have to view everything from the proper stance. Your point of view is the difference between allowing it to be a stress-relieving form of entertainment and viewing it as a form of reality with harmful consequences. But even worse, it can become an influential voice. We must discover how things affect us spiritually as we choose our entertainment, news, and other media formats.

If we're watching breaking news, we shouldn't view it as an impressionable student. A safer angle would be as a parent listening to a child. When we observe with this approach, we understand that the child's interpretation may not be accurate. We also know that the child may embellish. We understand that the child may fabricate the story to persuade us. But, most importantly, we know that the whole issue may be manufactured from start to finish.

That's how we should approach anything we didn't create or witness first-hand. Our minds should be open to hearing but not free to accept everything offered. Although closing our minds is considered harmful, we must be cautious to see how things affect us. We should open our minds to information without letting it overwhelm us spiritually. The danger in accepting things without caution is that we're storing flawed information we may rely on in the future.

Collective Influence

We see the impact of our physical actions, but our effect on life is more remarkable than simple physical activity. The ideas we've accepted show up in our behavior. That becomes part of our impact on the world. The influence we choose to take is remarkable, and we should acknowledge the effect it produces. We exercise this personal power daily, and our collective impact on life is displayed through every event recorded in human history. The foundation for our impact in life is rooted in our answers to the calls we receive.

Throughout history, leaders have elevated themselves into powerful positions over nations and empires. Several of these figures spread confusion and chaos, leading to destruction within their borders, but a few reached out to impact the world. Some of the more familiar dictators include the tyrants who rose to power and initiated the events that led to our world wars. Still, there have been many others throughout history. Although these leaders were the spark for the carnage, they didn't perform the widespread devastation themselves. They inspired the destruction and carnage, but individuals performed the acts. They accepted the negative influence, disregarded humanity, and answered the call to action. That is the impact when we don't recognize the power that exists when we answer calls. It's also the result of not honoring that power's collective impact. However, the leaders of these movements understood it extensively.

Dictators can't rise to control a nation without support. They require followers to accept the vision and establish it in their lives. Every idea requires human representation to manifest into reality. You and I are that representation. We are the force that brings concepts to reality by answering the calls. That is the vital importance and power that every human being owns.

If our existence has a purpose, this responsibility must be a significant part of that purpose. We have the power to create and sustain the ideologies and concepts that dominate our minds and impact the world. That enormous responsibility is overlooked when masked by the issues, burdens, needs, and desires that overwhelm us.

If we aren't vigilant in performing this duty, we will apply our power in ways that may unintentionally harm our personal lives and the external world. The dictators of the past represent the same types of influences we have in our individual lives. The activity may not be as extreme, but the impact on you is comparable. We can learn from the events of our collective history and find similar influences that cause frustration in our personal lives today.

Insufficient Coverage

Chapter 10

The Misinformation Multiplier

Artificial Intelligence Is Calling

The fight for your attention is intense. Websites track your searches and compile data to maximize their efforts to discover your patterns. They overwhelm you with ads and pop-ups that can lead you astray. Instead of tossing information and propaganda in front of random groups, today's callers are more specific and personal. They can compile enough personal data to know exactly how to approach you with their sales pitch. As a result, the need to take command of your awareness has never been more critical.

Although the impact from each call remains the same as in the past, artificial intelligence is a misinformation and manipulation multiplier. The exploitation, biases, and falsification we experience are increasing daily. Those who understand the incredible value of grasping our attention are finding unique methods to capture it. That's important because issues that grab our attention own our lives. It's true even if each only holds you for a brief period. That short period could have a profound effect. The attack on our attention doesn't respect our wellness. It only wants us to discover and cling to a proposal. It intends to disrupt our presence and shift our outlook. That shift can result in significant differences in how we conduct our lives.

Obligated to Create

We're born into a unique relationship that overshadows every partnership that exists. The arrangement allows us to live freely, but we must contribute to life through our presence while we're here. Everything we say, do, or fail to do is our contribution and impacts life. This requirement to constantly impact life in exchange for our existence is absolute. We're unrestricted in what we offer in return for existing. Life doesn't tell us how to give back, what to give, or who to give to daily. We're allowed to make our impression without limitations on expressing ourselves.

Your life is a form of currency that you can invest anywhere you choose. This currency allows you to implement actions and release ideas that alter the world in tiny or massive ways. It enables us to convert thoughts, ideas, and concepts into reality. Every innovation forms through this process. Two limitations come with this currency. First, you can't stash the currency away to use it on a rainy day. You have to spend it every day in the present moment. The second is that your acts are irreversible. You can apologize and change your behavior, but life won't undo what you initially invested your currency in. You can make amends as you move forward to atone for your missteps. That's how we learn, grow, and positively impact life.

No one exists without having an impact on life. Even the unborn child affects the mother, father, and others before the child enters the world. We might say that some people have a broader impact than others, but we'll never know the total impact that any individual presents. But we know for a fact that every life has an effect. The most poverty-stricken person on the planet is affecting society's economic situation. That position represents a contribution from their presence. We might say they aren't contributing to life, but we'd be wrong. We contribute by what we give and what we fail to contribute to life. The impoverished person doesn't contribute to many detrimental factors that others openly deposit into daily. They don't participate in many harmful ways that we impact the Earth's environment, yet most of us do. We dismiss our contribution as the lesser of the many evils, but any contribution to a "negative" has a consequence.

Every act, from a simple smile to a step on the moon, has an impact. It's our offering to life in exchange for living. Our lives are the conduit that brings concepts to reality. Life doesn't require you to be creative to change things you encounter. You just have to be alive. Others can use your life to establish something they value if you let them. Instead of using their creativity to build their concept, they use their imagination to get you to make it for them. They may even financially compensate you for using your life currency towards their idea. Regardless of the compensation, it will never be worth the currency you expanded because your human currency is priceless.

Global Coverage

We can never forget how dictators were able to move entire nations by influencing segments of their populations. The horrible acts that occurred in the process are attributed to the leaders even though they didn't perform the actions. They carried a destructive essence within and spread it to others through manipulation. We must remember that the average citizen accepted the influence and conducted the deadly acts. We are those people.

Historical records attempt to document the facts, but we must go deeper into the facts to discover the forces that caused the actions. We can then understand how people allowed themselves to carry out the inhumane plans their leaders conceptualized. We can identify moments that were available to reject the destructive influences. We can establish an inner conviction so that these types of ideologies never again progress into reality.

When fear becomes the emotion that dominates our state of being, it can guide our perspective. Our decisions born in that state may be inappropriate. Someone may have introduced the source behind the fear we're experiencing. When we move without awareness, we answer calls without objectivity. A persistent voice can persuade an individual, a group, or even an entire nation, even when the intent is destructive. If that voice makes a personal connection and gains a large enough platform, it becomes even more powerful. It can cause individual disagreements or lead to hatred, violence, and wars between nations. We must develop an intimate relationship with our awareness to ensure we aren't moving under someone else's ill-advised will.

Every caller's target is our human currency when trying to help or hurt us. They approach our intelligence, emotions, and senses, but their goal is to modify our perspective. Then, they can convince us to redirect how and where we invest our currency. The angle they want you to accept could be beneficial, but your awareness must be intact to determine the impact on your life.

Science has proven many ways we physically alter life, but we also impact through the influence we give and receive. Just as materials can destroy our planet, negative influences on the human spirit can also oppress our existence. It can dismantle us collectively, or it can wreak havoc on an individual life. The power to influence the human spirit and our acceptance of the influence that others provide is potent. We can't find evidence in an experiment because the attraction is spiritual, but the results from influences are life-altering.

Spirit Bullies

Bullies have always had a bad reputation. We recognize them by their attempts to intimidate, coerce, or cause harm. They look for ways to apply pressure on their victims and use that power to achieve their objectives. They know how to overpower with force, but the most dangerous bullies are nontraditional. They know how to target the spirit without physical contact. Many don't need you to fear them; their goal is to exploit you for their gain. That gain could be financial, but their true objective may be hard to discover.

Have you ever spoken with someone who wouldn't consider your point of view in the conversation? They may exceed disagreeing with you by desiring to force their viewpoint on you. Or maybe you've encountered someone experiencing disappointment or a setback in their life, and they constantly attack others. These are a couple of examples of spiritual bullies, but they take on many different forms in your life. A spiritual bully is someone whose goal is to subdue your spirit, attitude, and presence. They attempt to alter your being by providing words and actions that attack your spirit.

Identifying the reason for their attack shouldn't be your primary concern. Your priority must be protecting your presence. Since many bullies are people you have personal or professional relationships with, you may not recognize their tactics because you've come to accept their behavior. But before you continue to answer their calls, you need to consider the effect on your being. You have to protect yourself from voluntarily falling into the negative state they're offering.

You can't foster a fruitful relationship by overpowering others or allowing them to dominate you. Some people may attempt to push an opinion on you by force. They want you to concede to their view; if not, they'll find alternate methods to ruin your spirit. Often, they don't even hear your point of view or care about your desire. They've already closed off any chance of seeing things any other way or allowing you to have your own opinion. They aren't interested in accepting anything that isn't in line with their convictions, but they won't simply let you be at ease. They want to ruin your presence, so they attack you spiritually. Spiritual bullies wish to force their opinions without regard for yours. Some only want you to accept their point so it will influence your actions.

If you allow yourself to fall into battle with spiritual bullies, the only person you'll hurt is yourself. You can't blame others for your essence, but they can alter your spirit when you're preoccupied. Going to battle with a spiritual bully always results in a loss. Not because you can't make them see your point of view but because fighting them is a spiritual and emotional loss. You can only win with indifference to them. Any energy put forth in a personal battle with them is an automatic loss for you.

Some people are skilled at lighting fires and walking away. Their victims waste precious time trying to extinguish the flames in their own lives. The aggressor likely has tons of experience. The victim is left to find a way to get through the situation. Any time used to recover from a battle wastes time and energy. While the other person is thriving, you struggle from the encounter. The lasting impact is the real danger of sparring with spiritual bullies.

Disadvantage

We all have different personalities, strengths and weaknesses, and unique responses. Some of us manage certain stressful situations effortlessly but struggle in other circumstances. Our varied responses show the danger of battling with people who invite confrontations. Some may be well-versed and prepared to oppose others. They may be able to fight with people all day. They move from one scenario to the next, fully capable of remaining focused. However, the people they battle with may be unable to do that easily.

Some people can't argue and move forward without lasting effects. The confrontation could cause harm for the remainder of that day, month, or even the rest of their life. The impact of choosing to battle with argumentative people can be lasting. The aggressor might be able to drop it as soon as the conversation ends. They can continue with their day without missing a beat. The victim remains emotionally trapped.

When a spiritual bully attacks, all aspects of your life become vulnerable. Your ability to move with clarity suffers because of the destructive encounter. The most effective way of dealing with the spiritual bully is to be indifferent to their attack on you. They'll want to engage you and attack in other ways, but you must be aware of their efforts to draw you into battle. It's not your responsibility to prove you're right in the situation. Your responsibility is to ensure you protect yourself from anything with destructive potential. You're not playing a game against them. The only victory you seek is to remain in a state of clarity that will drive you toward your peace. Your ego may want to pursue the fight with a bully, but you have to remain in control.

Why is this important? Because so often in life, the ones that do the most damage to us are the ones closest to us. We might complain about our boss, the government, or many other things, but the ones that affect us deeply are much closer to home. A loved one can say something that can instantly deflate your spirit. That deflated spirit can attach to thoughts and actions that may counter your intentions and well-being.

Disconnecting the Message

When someone speaks to you intending to move your spirit, you can refuse to connect it to your being. Unfortunately, we don't exercise this power. That might appear to be a small gesture to some, but it can enormously impact you and the other person. We automatically honor spoken words, especially when they come from someone we love, respect, or recognize through familiarity. This spiritual acceptance is the birthplace of many of the problems that we experience.

Our acceptance allows words to affect our presence. Surprisingly, we don't allow words of motivation to give us that type of long-term inspiration. Inspirational words may ignite us for a moment; then, we return to the patterns we've come to accept. You can't deny that you heard the words, but you command the way these words affect your being. That's within your spiritual power.

When you're more protective of your spirit, you won't automatically give life to the words that others say. You should even exercise caution with the ones you love more than anyone else. So many times, we question our own words, but we automatically honor the things others say. When you give up your ability to decline someone's authority, you open yourself to mental and physical bias and abuse. We see this constantly on the Internet, in the news, and within our network of friends and family. Your preferences are cast aside, and you operate from a state you didn't intend. We shouldn't spiritually accept another's words without knowing what we acquire. These attachments can quickly become adverse actions that alter our presence and world.

Insufficient Coverage

Chapter 11

Favorites

Intimate Callers with Influence

The impact from intimate callers is as powerful as any call. These calls are troublesome because you initiate or at least have a hand in reviving them in your awareness. They arrive as thoughts and feelings that seem to appear from nowhere, but every call has a source. You received the call in the past, but it affects your awareness when something causes you to reflect on it. The emotions that arise point to something we've been overlooking. Here are a few examples of personal callers that influence our presence.

1. Habits

Some things positively impact you and are inspiring, while others create disharmony. You must become aware of how things are affecting your life. You have to determine how your routines and habits are touching you because the impact can damage your presence. You could list habits considered wasteful or harmful, but that list would only apply to you. We can't label someone else's practices without knowing how those habits alter that specific person's being. Some habits are detrimental to our well-being, so we must attempt to drop them. But something wrong for one person could provide the relief someone else requires. You have to assess how your habits are affecting you spiritually. Then, you can determine if you should continue or stop it. When your habit is dangerous but feels uplifting, you need to face reality. If the facts state that it's harmful, others are warning you of the danger, and you know that it's causing problems you have to stop ignoring the truth. Take the time and make the commitment to remove and replace it. But before you do anything, settle it internally.

2. Self-Created Purpose

A primary distraction is a belief that our self-discovered purpose is our primary reason for living. Although our chosen purpose may positively contribute to life, it doesn't overshadow the natural impact we already offer. When we pour all our effort into our self-proclaimed reason for living, we may be overlooking the fact that we already influence life through our daily presence. We press forward with our self-proclaimed purpose without realizing the impact we already present. Acknowledging our actual purpose allows you to positively impact life as you pursue and perform anything else you decide to claim as your purpose.

3. Dissatisfaction

Arguing and complaining are two of the most potent disruptions. Although we externalize them with our words, they initiate from emotions and thoughts that we advance. Having a discussion isn't the same as arguing or complaining. The approach we use to display our discomfort helps determine the impact on our presence. We have to ensure we understand the approach we're using because it's affecting our spirit.

When we argue, we try to convince others to see our point of view while the other person wants to defend theirs. This often causes the other person to move further away from seeing your point of view. They switch their attention from the subject of the argument to the ego trying to win. You may be doing the same thing. There are rarely winners in a fight. Both communicators lose when they close their minds to each other.

When we complain, we express our dissatisfaction with something. It may feel good to externalize that feeling, but we need to correct it before externalizing anything. Complaining is airing your frustrations to the environment, which may cause more problems. Complaints must be redirected to create motivation and inspiration. Then, you can move yourself out of the disturbing situation.

When we argue or complain about something that happened in the past, we're pressing the refresh button. Why would we want to renew a negative experience? When we complain about something we experienced, we need to question why we refuse to let it go.

4. History

Progress is impossible when there's a chain attaching you to your past. Your attachment to yesterday will never allow you to break free. It doesn't matter if your current life has anything to do with the past you're holding; its effect remains the same. That spiritual effect can be crippling. Memories can get in the way of your wellness. It will continue to disrupt your life until you release your attachment to it.

We don't have to forget our past events, but we should put them in their place. That place is anywhere but attached to your inner being. Your attachment to the injustices of the past can be a heavy burden that weighs on you as you try to move forward. Holding on to it is discouraging and you might release something new.

The thing you remove might be the desire, the dream, or the new person you want to become.

We might be able to accomplish our goals in life but still not have the ability to release that excess baggage of our past. Eventually, we'll let something go. The easiest thing to remove is the thing we have the least attachment to. If you've been holding on to some pain for a long time, you won't let it go quickly. It will be easier to release the new attachment, our successes. You have less of a grip on it, even though it's what you desire to achieve.

5. Other People's Garbage

You often see people talking or texting on the phone throughout the day. Sometimes, you may even hear a part of the conversation. The person on the other end of the discussion receives all the data the sender uploads to them. The speaker may not consider what they're doing to the receiver during the interaction, but it could be deflating their spirit.

When communicating, you have to be cautious about what you're investing in. You can listen to everything but shouldn't invest in everything others offer you. They often don't know what they're doing to you and how they may harm your essence. You have to completely own your state of being because it is a full-time job. It's your responsibility and in your best interest to maintain your state of being. That doesn't mean we should only have concerns about ourselves.

We need to be supportive of others while sustaining our wellness.

6. What You Do for a Living

A giant distraction that can silently steal from your growth is your career. When you elevate your job above everything, you allow it to become the focal point of your life. Regardless of how essential you are at your job, your life is still the center of your world. The world won't stop turning when you no longer fill that position. That should indicate that your career shouldn't be the focal point of your existence. The focal point of your presence is your life, not what you do for a living. Though the world may love you for what you can provide, you're the focal point of your existence.

7. The Present Moment

The present allows us to view our situations from an alternative perspective. We can visualize and create a new reality to work toward at any time. Unfortunately, the present moment that we are experiencing is all too often depletive rather than creative. It's spiritually draining rather than supplying. We spend our time complaining and dwelling on the negative aspects of our situation rather than looking for positive solutions. The present is our only moment, so we must use it for growth, or it will steal away by default. There isn't much room for play within the boundaries of the present moment. It's either beneficial or it's wasted.

The Sources of Suffering

If we can get ahead of our interpretations, we can tame the inner enemy that's allowing external factors to dominate our presence. Our awareness can be an early detection system that alerts us before we open the door to faulty perspectives. These issues manifest into psychological and physical problems. Securing a positive outlook is the primary method to encourage a favorable evaluation of the present moment.

Too many of us are overly concerned with trivial events that are insignificant. We're already dealing with calls about situations within our families, at work, and other personal aspects. Then, we find ourselves immersed in politics, technological innovations, and irrelevant entertainment controversies that disturb our presence. We allow them to become the center of our attention and cause unnecessary disruptions. That clutter can affect our spirit based on our interpretation of events and how we relate them to our lives.

Something that uplifts your spirit could be the same thing that causes agony for others. An event that inspires most people won't necessarily have the same effect on you. Therefore, you must internally monitor your state of being as life sends you calls. That's the truth we fail to acknowledge when we try to correct problems. We all have areas we want to improve, but often, we struggle to make the improvements real. We notice the need to change; we commit to the new actions but eventually return to our old patterns. We often fail because we move into action without addressing the primary factor that oversees our activities. That principal factor is our spirit. A damaged spirit will deter our effort in any area we try to improve.

Your spirit has a direct effect on your physical world. Your creativity, performance, and well-being are all dependent on your mood. What can ruin your spirit? Anything! Just like anything can uplift it. It's up to you. Therefore, you must acknowledge and create a relationship with your spirituality. You can effectively manage your life when you understand how you're spiritually affected by people, situations, and events. You don't have to buy what the world is selling you.

There's a vast difference between those who find content and those who continue to struggle. Success isn't measured physically, and neither is happiness. You can experience success in your career, finances, and relationships yet live a deprived existence. That's because material progress doesn't equal satisfaction or happiness. But if you listen to society's voice, you'll mistakenly believe it does.

Your presence provides the ease and comfort you can possess, but it won't eliminate adversity. It prepares you to navigate through troubling times with the understanding that life continues. We associate a successful existence with financial abundance, career accomplishments, and beautiful relationships, but that's not the case. Spiritual comfort doesn't have any physical requirements. You can find comfort in places that most would consider unacceptable. This awareness is essential to discovering peace and achieving it daily. You don't have to display symbols of happiness to the world; you must find satisfaction and enjoyment with life spiritually within yourself.

Part Three

I Already Answered

I Already Answered

Chapter 12

Stronger,
If You Let It

What doesn't kill you makes you stronger. However, it could also lead you down a path of destruction. It all depends on how you internally manage it. Anything can harm your spirit, so you must protect yourself. When you allow problems to damage your spirit, the results can last indefinitely. You can find yourself in a pit of depression that might be difficult to recover from. That's why your presence is essential to recovering from disturbing calls.

If you allow things to touch you negatively, you'll likely respond harshly. When we openly allow everything to touch us deeper than the surface of our awareness, we risk emotional distress. Many of us take offense, feel disrespected, or react in a form of retaliation to what we experience while others can accept a personal attack without allowing it to arouse them. They maintain their presence, which causes them to bypass any harmful immediate retaliation. They remain grounded. That enables them to maintain self-control and abstain from regrettable actions. They can move forward with their creativity intact instead of responding with an angered spirit. They retain their presence, allowing them to remain in their chosen state of being instead of allowing others to pull them out of character. That skill can't be purchased with any amount of money.

Inner awareness is one of the most important aspects of life, but it isn't emphasized in our education or background. We internally process every situation that approaches us before reacting, but we don't slow down to observe this inner activity. We let things harm us and allow that to control our response. Inner awareness teaches you to respond without losing control.

Life forces you to try many different things to live an abundant life. The key to navigating the twists and turns is heightening your awareness. You need to determine when you're benefiting from what you're doing. When you aren't satisfied with your actions, you need the courage and faith to stop it and try something else.

You shouldn't continue to pursue a disturbing activity just because you've become comfortable with it. You cheat yourself out of the abundance life offers when you settle. You have to find a way to try everything you're driven towards that's healthy and enhances your wellness. When you discover something you enjoy, you add it to your life. When you identify something unaligned with your spirit, you drop it and move on to the next experience. Don't' linger in negativity because anything can become habitual. Clinging to things you disagree with can negatively affect other areas. When you finally release something detrimental, capture the lesson so you won't have to experience it again.

There's a fine line between allowing something to be as it is and deciding to remove it from your life. You need to discover how it is affecting you spiritually. Something that appears to be a waste of time could be the thing that inspires you and keeps you going. Do you believe you can create a more enjoyable experience by walking away from that thing? Maybe you feel you have to stay attached to it. If you think you have to remain connected, that's fine. At least you're seriously addressing things in your life. Maybe you'll learn that you can't distance yourself from it now. You realize you have to work on that situation. You can grow and eventually create a more exceptional experience from that scenario.

That's the key to most struggles in life. We need to identify issues, spiritually address them, and grow. We'll continue to face obstacles that challenge our confidence. You shouldn't run away from anything, but you don't sit around and let things get out of control. You must be prepared to walk away from anything with confidence. If you're not ready to walk, you have to build that confidence in yourself. You must create a situation that will allow you to deal with discomfort until you can walk away confidently. That confidence is developed internally.

How can we build confidence in ourselves? We have to try different things! We must discover what we enjoy, delete what we don't, and move on. We must create enjoyable experiences that build us up rather than tear us down in situations we can't alter. We should acknowledge things that make us uncomfortable. Once we identify them, we can consciously face these aspects confidently instead of reluctantly. That's how we build the courage to answer our calls without fear and trepidation.

When we confront something, we can conquer it or try to understand our discomfort. You don't have to master everything in this world, but you need to know how to deal with the things you have to face. You have to give yourself the confidence to know how to face difficulty. More importantly, you learn how to approach matters that you aren't comfortable with in the future. That's the tremendous value gained when facing any uncomfortable areas of your life. That's how we become stronger.

When you revisit experiences, consider their total value, not just the joy or pain. Every event won't be positive. You could feel sorry for yourself or blame others for the experiences leading to your current circumstances. The best thing you can do is see the tremendous value of the wisdom you could gain from the situations.

There's no better teacher than life itself. Life is such a great teacher that it will continue to present the same lesson with slight variations until you grasp it. Then, it may continue to offer it to you to ensure you've become an expert in that area. Ask anyone who's stepped away from an addiction that was negatively affecting them. Every day, they receive calls proposing a return to that addiction. Life doesn't eliminate the thing that is the source of the addiction. Your wisdom from the experiences will allow you to move forward.

This is the view we need to take when observing the past. This should be the stance we operate from as we continue our journey through life. When we work from this position, we understand that the current situation is not as desperate as it appears. It's simply another opportunity for growth in this never-ending schoolhouse called life.

You must become the most competent and aware person regarding your life. You have the best equipment to gauge your predicament. Everyone else is only guessing based on your actions. Your feelings and emotions are signals and warning signs for you. They're warning you of what's brewing and where you're heading spiritually.

Too much of a good feeling can even be a sign of caution. You have to determine the source and decide if it's best for your wellness. Your actions also tell you where you're heading, but they come up much later in the process. By the time you act, you've already gone through several layers of cautions and warnings that you could've identified. You can survive without learning math or science, but your daily life will be an internal struggle when you can't identify the signs and signals warning you about your well-being.

Chapter 13

Choosing A New Provider

We must become conscious of our freedom to direct our lives. If we don't, others will use us to enrich their lives at our expense. So why not focus on improving our own wellness? Our awareness can be our guide. We may find that others have been asking us to take a back seat while they drive the bus. When you notice that the bus they are trying to drive has your name on it, you have to take control of it.

Life is too short to be a passenger on your bus, but that's what you may be accepting. You may know someone who walks with their chest out and their head high with pride. That's not how you have to move physically, but it's the feeling you must take when it comes to your existence. You must remember that you are influencing the world with everything you do. If you move with an unpleasant essence, your actions will be harmful instead of uplifting. No one can claim they have command over you in life. They should have that presence about their existence; you must also have it about yours.

When you face troubling situations, you could try to evade them. However, that may not be a healthy or realistic possibility. You can try blocking them out of your mind, but that's never an acceptable option either. Many things we struggle with are part of our daily lives and can't be avoided. Acknowledging the issue without spiritually investing in it is the best option to prevent the situation from causing damage. When we invest, we devote all our inner resources. That leads to overthinking, worrying, and anxiety. We must learn to address our issues the best way we can and press forward. The best way forward is to settle with it internally before acting.

Prolonged Fallout

When we have a negative encounter with someone, we often dwell on it longer than we should. We tell our partner, family, and friends about the encounter, so they know what we experienced. Although it is essential to communicate and share our lives with others, we must exercise caution in how we express our experiences. We can easily allow simple conversations to create attachments that bind us to negative states of being. That creates more harm than we initially encountered.

If you're voicing the problem, you're living from that angle. You're in a completely different space if you're discussing your actions that can resolve the issue. You can discover your point of focus through your conversations. Your focus must turn to embracing the solution, not the problem. You shouldn't invest in the negativity that arises when you encounter or discuss the situation. When the negativity surfaces, you can't allow yourself to become aroused and continue to feed off it.

Often, we allow ourselves to live in the feelings and emotions arising from our issues. We allow it to become a part of our identity. That could be a huge mistake. We could be internally investing in something that will encourage unproductive thoughts and destructive actions. Acknowledgment without attachment is a more effective form of managing life when you don't have physical control.

Time For a Change

Your awareness also offers the presence to know when it's time to move on from something in your life. So many times, we find ourselves clinging to things that no longer offer us a healthy diet. When we stay in areas that aren't healthy, we deny the progress awaiting us. You have to determine if your present conditions are properly feeding you or if you require a new diet. Everything in life is on the menu. You need to recognize that because opportunities uplift or weaken your resolve.

When considering a change, our awareness will ensure we aren't running away from something we need to address. We can't advance by running away. That uneasy, disheartening, fearful, or anxious feeling is warning you that you need to confront an issue. We can only move forward by addressing our circumstances. After resolving positively or negatively, that growth can move us to a different objective. That's what's supposed to happen when we're experiencing growth and expansion.

Subconscious Cooperation

We continue to impact life as we deal with the issues that confront us personally. However, while focusing on our concerns, we may neglect that we always influence life through our responses to everyday situations. If we could see the intangible impact of our actions, we might begin to see the priceless value and importance that every life holds. We'd see that our support fuels every rise to power. That rise to power may be on a global level, circumstances at your place of employment, or someone's ability to influence a situation in your personal life. If we adopt a new perspective, we can discover the positive and negative ways we affect our lives. Then, we set out to impact the world.

It's easy to look back in history and criticize the people who allowed the various dictators and tyrants to gain power. But we aren't experiencing the conditions they faced. Just as they accepted unfortunate influences, we may be allowing things to manifest today that negatively impact our world. If we could go back and question the people about the methods used, such as torture, rape, mass killings, or genocide, they would likely tell you they weren't aware of those tactics, and they wouldn't have supported it. Yet, they endorsed the leaders who used those methods, and their peers applied the activities to reality.

The dictators of the past manipulated their followers into accepting their visions by targeting public opinion. They promised to improve the issues that confronted people personally. That historically involved placing blame on segments of society they promoted as the source of the problems. Like the scam caller who doesn't reveal the impact of his influence, these dictators sold a corrupted vision in exchange for a spiritual commitment. They convinced citizens to accept that vision and ultimately deliver trauma on their neighbors without regard for life. The leaders didn't create ill will between the diverse groups; they capitalized on subtle beliefs and prejudices already existing in society and expanded them. These leaders recognized the importance of securing the community's trust first, then inspiring hostility in the minds of the people they seduced. Without the people's support, these rulers' aspirations would never have become a reality. Their dominance depended on the people's answers to the calls they sent out.

Triggering the Soul

The hardships and struggles of life meet us physically and mentally but always affect us spiritually. It displays in our emotions and feelings but manifests through our actions. Influential leaders, just like scammers, understand this inner activity. They know how to influence it and use that power to energize their initiatives, positively or negatively. They use the social and economic struggles that every society experiences to touch individuals personally. They use clever slogans and catchphrases to arouse their targets. Once the masses are inspired, a slight nudge is powerful enough to move their visions to reality. Once inspired, people begin to place more energy toward that spark. They may not even consider the primary or secondhand effect on others.

The human spirit has always been the factor that allows initiatives to advance. If we aren't spiritually inspired to move, accomplishing goals won't be easy. These dictators used the power in that spirit to bring their atrocious visions to reality. First, they created an enemy to blame society's problems on, then inspired people to unite against that falsely accused segment of society. Once in power, they continued to target the spirit to move their initiatives forward.

When we fail to see the enormous impact that comes with our lives, we disrespect the natural power that accompanies life. The irrelevant position many of us spiritually place ourselves in leads to a longing to be a part of something greater. That exposes us to influences that replace that feeling of insignificance. When others target that insecurity, there's no limit to the power they can obtain. We believe we have to sit in a powerful position to possess a high level of responsibility. We don't realize that our birth already placed us in that position. We continuously allow others to influence our lives without understanding the impact.

Yesterday, Today, & Tomorrow

We're no different from those who faced the influence of yesterday's menacing dictators. We continue to face life's daily challenges in society, but we receive them in new forms due to advancements in technology and information. Unfortunately, many of us don't have a conscious relationship with our spiritual nature to notice what's occurring below the physical surface.

We allow aspects that we consider normal to manipulate and dominate our lives, which, in turn, dominates our spirit. Thus, we surrender our best opportunity to view our impact from within before we act. Ultimately, our acts contribute to the situations in our lives and throughout the world. We surrender our power to impact life positively because of the burdens and struggles overwhelming our personal lives.

We support many ideas presented to us without questioning the full impact. Unfortunately, some of the notions we accept aren't healthy and produce long-term problems. Unfortunately, we can't quickly identify the origins because they're deeply embedded. But they're all recoverable if we're determined to find them. We can find our hidden effects on situations through our awareness. It offers a conscious observation of things influencing us within our souls. It displays the impact of that influence when we apply it in the world through our physical actions and beyond. When we use awareness, we can detect the forces moving us to stop the adverse effects we're distributing into the world.

Voluntary Participation

Casually accepting the influences our environment offers is a hazardous practice. The various roles we're offered to play throughout our lives can lead to severe problems when we allow them to dominate our essence. As a parent, you're expected to display specific characteristics your culture defines. Your occupation also has traits you accept to fill the position. You assume so many different roles throughout the day that you don't even recognize the transition from one to the next. Although our roles begin as simple positions in relationships or in society in general, they come with traits we attach to our being. While these traits are appropriate in that specific position, they can become hazardous to our essence when we allow them to displace our presence.

As you adopt these traits, the line between the being you are and the part you play can become blurred. You can become the product of the characteristics of the positions. That's one of the many ways we allow the world to shape us instead of directing our lives. We can become pawns without recognizing our voluntary participation.

If we looked closer at our responses to everything we face, we would discover that our inner presence significantly contributes to our circumstances. The consequences we face from our actions become the situations that make up our daily lives. Those actions come from our state of being. We allow our roles, the environment, and others we've anointed as authority figures to manipulate, influence, and dominate our spirit, which can cause us to alter our actions.

We're already emotionally responding to everything we face without acknowledging it. This inner response sets our answer to the call in motion. We need to recognize this activity because it has a tremendous effect. The mini tyrants and micro dictators in our lives tremendously influence our essence. Although we're expected to respect many of them because of their positions, we shouldn't adopt or sustain their ideals and beliefs without question. At some point in our lives, we must exercise our free will to reject the influence we face. Our state of being is our best opportunity to fix anything before we act on it. If we aren't moving from a favorable state of being, our actions can be detrimental.

Because our actions reveal immediate results, we believe altering them will resolve our issues. Although we must act to address our problems, we shouldn't do so before internally observing our situations. Our actions might help at the moment, but there's always an aspect we overlook that could be a source that lingers. The core of our issue remains active because it lives within our being. We must learn to approach our spirit as we seek solutions because it's always an active participant. Resolving an external problem may conceal an injured inner trigger that remains intact and ready to inflict harm in the future. When a similar call returns, our response will place us back in that unfortunate scenario.

Unseen Influences

Our presence is the soil in which our thoughts and actions are rooted. It's also an aspect that helps direct our steps. Looking at where you are in life and where the world is collectively, you'll see how we create circumstances that lead to the scenarios we experience. Our actions always come from our mental and spiritual states of being.

The spiritual impact of everything we encounter has a powerful effect. That effect is enhanced because it's not easily recognizable. When an event occurs, we can easily point to that specific event as a cause of a physical issue. When something impacts our presence, it's not so easy to identify the cause. As we interact with interesting people and amazing technology that attracts our senses, we forget to monitor the influences affecting our spirit. That's a dangerous oversight because the unseen influences attached to our being always impact other areas of our lives. That creates baggage that will be hard to identify.

Life continues to find ways to bring this influence to our attention. You can seek to discover it or learn through life's experiences. When forced into discovering it, it comes through eye-opening events. They can prompt us to look at life from a new perspective. But it remains up to us to accept the responsibility to use that new understanding as we move forward.

Internal or Public

We often see entertainers and politicians apologizing and promising to be better after they come under public scrutiny. Although their words are directed at the public, the action must occur internally. They'll allow the incident to alter their outlook and behavior or send out a public call for forgiveness to allude being canceled. In the first case, they've accepted life's voice and decided to change. In the other case, they've also heard the voice but decided to repair their image rather than address the internal source.

We encounter similar situations in our lives. Instead of being canceled by the public, we're trying to avoid cancellations by loved ones, friends, employers, coworkers, clients, and others. When we do something that offends others, we could find ourselves in an uncomfortable scenario. Just like the public figure, we can adjust our being or externally manipulate the situation. One option could resolve the problem but allow the inner source to remain untouched. The other will allow the growth needed to reduce or eliminate the behavior.

We heavily rely on our physical ability to maneuver everything we encounter. But we shouldn't neglect our ability to discover beyond that. We must learn to use our senses in conjunction with our awareness to identify the need for change. It's not a matter of choosing inner awareness over spatial awareness. They both have a significant role in navigating life, and we must learn to use them as one.

Invisible Touches

Our presence is the soil that nourishes our thoughts and actions. It's also the aspect that moves an individual, a community, a nation, and the world on its current course. Looking at where you are as an individual and where the world is, you'll see how we spiritually create many circumstances through our reactions to life. Events touch us physically, mentally, and emotionally, but regardless of how things find us, they always touch our souls. That touch affects how we see the world and our state of being.

Although not apparent, aren't most of our reactions based on our personal acceptance of an event? When we have an emotional response, doesn't it come from how something touched our soul? We often attack ourselves for being too emotional, but that emotional response comes from our current state of being. We aren't being too emotional; we're externally responding to emotions with our words and actions. When we know that our reactions create undesirable conditions, we must learn how to adjust them. But we shouldn't try to change without addressing our state of being.

Our emotions are trying to tell us something about our state of being. Instead of using our emotions as internal warning signs, we use them to trigger verbal and physical responses. Many times, these responses are ill-advised. Any response before a spiritual understanding of our feelings is a wasted opportunity.

Wellness In Your World

We should always go to the source, which is our spirit. We'll never discover the effect on our activities if we don't link our actions to the states that generate them. We'll continue to attempt to improve ourselves and correct situations without addressing the source, our spirit.

Many of us engage in activities supporting wellness, such as meditation, yoga, and prayer. Unfortunately, we don't allow the awareness and feeling these activities create to become prevalent in our lives. When we complete the physical aspects of our wellness practice, we brush off the focused consciousness it created and return to "reality" as we left it when we received a call.

That abandonment causes us to return to the limited view we're functioning with. We eliminate our broadened outlook from within and return to the narrow external position we've accepted. These same perspectives bind us to the recurring themes that have become routine. When we allow emotion to spark a response, we should see that we've abandoned the well-being we sought in our wellness exercise.

Observing our immediate reactions is the easiest and most revealing way to discover our unfiltered stance. Those innate responses show the immediate feelings we have towards that subject. We must be cautious when evaluating physical responses because the things we say and responses we take are not always the true expression of our inner beliefs. They are often the results of the roles we play in life or the environment we're currently occupying. The same scenario unfolding in a different setting may spark a different physical reaction.

Our actual response comes before any physical action we take. It can be challenging to discover it because we've become engrossed in the various roles we play. We become so great at playing them that we even fool ourselves with the automatic actions accompanying them. But the truth is always revealed by an inner reaction before any physical response. You're the only one who experiences that internal reaction.

If you desire to get to any truth concerning an issue in your life, you must learn to downgrade reliance on physical responses. Instead, you must observe the inner reactions that arrive before your physical response. You will notice that before you physically respond, you process your current role and factor that in. Truth always comes before any physical response. That's where answers to your truth live.

Clear Perspective

There is significant value in the information we can gather from an unbiased observation of our inner reactions. It reveals our current understanding before we adjust it to suit our roles or any environmental influences. When we can identify this untainted internal perspective, we can respond objectively. We can release our current views (if only for the moment) and become positive influences in life. That's how we can get around the noble or lowly opinion of ourselves and establish an authentic foundation to live by. THIS IS INNER AWARENESS. Without this level of self-analysis, we will continue to influence life with the biased perspectives we own.

When you identify negative influences, you can research other areas that may also be affected. Then, you can restructure different areas of your life on your terms. You can remove the baggage you've used as truth to establish a more candid reality. But this is a delicate exercise because you could also rearrange your perspective to make it even more unbalanced than before. Although biases exist in you and may never end, you can learn to acknowledge them without allowing them to alter your impact in life. You can allow others to be biased and partisan while maintaining your neutrality. When you have to choose a side, you make your choice without adding to the hysteria that may exist. It would help if you tried to become centered with an impartial perspective that doesn't allow material aspects or external influences to alter your being. THIS IS INNER AWARENESS.

Awareness shows us precisely what we create within ourselves and how it affects our lives. It also displays how that activity goes out to impact the world. We create problems and solutions, build bridges and obstacles, and create friends and enemies from our being. The effect of our creations reinforces that state of being within and then goes out into the world.

Any turbulence we create disrupts our peace, and that disruption carries over into the world through our lives. Conversely, any stability we create will also spill over and create stability in the external world through our presence. In this way, we can see how we individually contribute positively or negatively to the Oneness of humanity.

Presence

Inner awareness requires a presence that should drive our physical activities. Unfortunately, most of us function in the opposite direction. When physical aspects guide our spirit, we become the perfect victims of circumstances. If things are going well, we find ourselves spiritually uplifted, but we fall into a rut when things are down. Some people understand this and won't proceed with important activities when they don't feel right. Instead, they'll delay a scheduled event until they reach a better state. During this delay, they'll do whatever they need to improve their spirit. Some meditate, practice yoga, go for a walk, retreat to solitude, or find another means to get themselves spiritually aligned. They know their inner feelings and well-being enormously impact the results they will obtain.

We always consider our mental and physical health when considering our well-being. However, we fail to question how our attitude and spirit affect our health. Although they aren't visible, they are a significant factor in how we create, sustain, or dissolve predicaments. Every original impression we leave on the world is rooted in our spiritual state. All others originate externally, but we supply them to the world through our being. When someone's influence causes you to act, you've used your life for someone else's benefit. That can be helpful and may be beneficial for you, but you have to be aware of the effect of your actions to ensure you are delivering a positive effect.

The power of your presence stimulates positive transformation, encourages stagnation, or speeds up our decline. It quietly lifts you to greater heights or lowers you to repeated depths of disappointment. It provides an internal explanation for our successes and our setbacks. This understanding reduces our tendency to externalize the cause of our circumstances. Instead, we accept responsibility and embrace it. It introduces us to our internal relationship with everyone and everything we face, which determines how we choose to interact.

Our contributions to life are always spirited but not necessarily rooted in our own spirit. All thoughts need a human life to materialize in the world. The more lives that accept it, the more significant the impact. Although our actions give concrete proof of how we are affecting life, those actions are always rooted in someone's being. Therefore, you must ensure that your impressions in life are rooted in your spirit. You may be impacting life based on influence intended to exploit something instead of the natural influence life offers. Natural influences emerge; others are staged and prepared by an external source to persuade your behavior for your benefit or detriment.

Regardless of what you do in life, there's one purpose that we're all destined to fill. That purpose is to impact life and influence the world through our presence. As technology advances, we find that our individual voices have greater reach and a larger impact than ever. Therefore, we must ensure that our lasting impressions are internally developed and not adversely influenced by external sources. The way we reach out and touch others reveals our legacy. From there, it's the way we move humanity. That's what defines our minutes, days, and, ultimately, our entire existence, positively or negatively.

I Already Answered

Chapter 14

Subtle Actions

Sometimes, it feels that you're simply moving through life without purpose. Nothing could be further from the truth. Everything you do affects life, both yours and the lives of those around you. That's why your answer to calls is so impactful. Every act has an effect. Even the smallest act of kindness or anger is powerful. When we fail to recognize our impact, we lose another chance to influence life positively. But if we wait a moment, another opportunity arises.

In the 1960s, psychologist Stanley Milgram investigated a theory known as the small world problem. This idea suggested that a small number of intermediaries could link any two people. His research found that an average of only five to six intermediaries separated most people. In other words, we're all within six relationships from connecting with anyone. We have to make the right connections. Since Milgram's experiments, other institutions have used modern techniques to test the theory further. The Internet, email, and other digitally based systems have also been used to test the theory. This modern testing also supports the idea. The actual number of intermediaries isn't important. What is eye-opening is the relatively close human connections that exist in our world even before the digital age.

If we're so closely networked through personal relationships, imagine the vast networks we form through our shared beliefs, concepts, and ideologies. We internally cling to our ideologies like prized possessions. We keep them alive through our associations, relationships, and other affiliations. We also preserve them through our simple conversations and subtle behaviors. We instinctively move in alignment with our beliefs even when we aren't actively voicing them. Our allegiance to these ideologies forms networks with others who adhere to similar beliefs without requiring direct communication.

These bonding networks don't require a digital means of transmission. They survive and expand in the way they've always endured. These ideas live and travel through human transactions and survive through the people who adopt them. Social media and other digital technology have only increased their reach. These networks don't have any material qualities that allow them to be defined or measured, but they have a powerful effect as they lay dormant within the individuals. When the environment is ready and vulnerable, the holders of the ideas can shift reality through their actions. When many people engage in a belief that's dormant in the world but alive within the soul, it can take the environment by storm when it eventually unfolds. These invisible webs of connectivity play a critical role in the state of our communities and ultimately can affect everyone.

Although we live in a world dominated by actions, we can't ignore this invisible reality and its effects. People witness our acts, but our impact exceeds actions. We'll continue to populate the world with the concepts and ideologies that change our lives. We inspire the beauty of philanthropy and goodwill but also generate disruption through everything from greed to injustice. Many of the hurtful and hateful concepts that exist have to be deliberately taught to the next generation. The owners of these hateful ideas teach the concepts by giving flawed, biased, and misguided examples as proof of their irresponsible guidance. They allow their adverse experiences to influence others without regard for the impact of their influence. Yet, we remain responsible for every idea that survives.

We're here to animate the world, and we do it without effort. When you neglect your position as an active participant, you'll never discover your actual contributions to life because most of them aren't material. You'll remain focused on accumulating knowledge, increasing your wealth, and creating a lifestyle that's been sold as desirable. Your focus will remain on the measurable successes and shortcomings that are associated with those aspects. In the meantime, you'll fail to see the infinite ways you impact your world as you chase your dream life. Pursuing greatness is not a problem. But neglecting to monitor the impact on our mental and spiritual presence from what you're accepting along the way is detrimental for both.

The essence we create through our actions outlines our imprint on the world, and the spirit or impact of our actions exceeds the acts. That effect lives within you and moves through those who witness and are affected by your words and actions. Social media and technology may have increased the reach, but connections have always existed. The way our actions are accepted always influences others. That influence sparks thoughts and actions in others that cause even more influence.

We've been led to believe that our purpose in life must be a noble calling, such as reducing global warming or creating the most prominent e-commerce business. But instead of solely focusing on measurable aspects, you should also consider your more profound impact. Every day, you awaken and illustrate life based on your outlook. You go about your day thinking and acting based on that stance. Your actions influence others, and they respond to your input. You do the same based on their input. We affect each other through our ideologies and beliefs without grandstanding to the public and announcing our stances. Instead, we express

it through our being and our subtle actions. We help create the torture that some people live within or the heaven that keeps them afloat. If we don't monitor our awareness, we could accept and unwittingly promote the hatred that others are spreading. We will continue to live with the unfortunate fallout from accepting faulty and negative influences and allowing them to poison the environment.

You'll never have more impact on the world than you already have! You may adopt a wider audience by accessing a larger platform, but that doesn't alter the spiritual effect you already place on the world. That might be surprising because you likely don't see it. Every time you express yourself through thoughts, words, and actions, you influence life. With the vast hidden networks that transmit our influence, there is no greater impact on life.

The weight of the world you experience in your material life is minimal compared to our heavy mental load. Yet, we carry this assignment without acknowledging it throughout our lives. It's a duty we're born to fulfill, and we can't escape it, but we tend to overlook it. When we neglect this responsibility, we allow others to direct it for us. Allowing others to control your input in life creates psychological disturbances that are difficult to identify because they're disguised. When we surrender control of our actions, we're destined to have internal problems that require help. Many of us have never taken the responsibility to control our awareness because we've been accepting everything we're fed. But, when we continue down this path, we accept abnormal behavior simply because others have accepted it.

In addition to the Small World Experiment, Stanley Milgram was also the author of a study concerning our behavior when we're under pressure to perform tasks. In this experiment, he tasked the participants to give electric shocks to an unseen "student" when they answered questions incorrectly. The hidden student verbally expressed severe pain and asked to end the punishment as the intensity of the shocks increased, but many participants continued to administer the shocks. Though it bothered some participants to continue delivering the shocks, over fifty percent did as they were instructed.

Milgram concluded that the participants felt compelled to continue the task with the understanding that they weren't directly responsible for the harm being delivered. They felt justified in continuing because they didn't feel responsible for the act. Yet if they hadn't administered the shock, it wouldn't have occurred. We can disassociate our responsibility from our actions, but life isn't concerned with human perception, obedience to authority, or the pressure to comply.

We might attempt to rationalize in an actual situation by stating that someone else would do it if we didn't. But life responds to the input you provide. In the case of the experiment, one input was the administered shock. The person who gave the orders may be ultimately responsible in human eyes, but reality responded to the participant's action. The individual who delivered the shock is responsible for the shock that manifested. We've learned to hide behind rules that protect us from civil or criminal prosecution. But life doesn't rely on a judicial interpretation of reality.

Life responds directly to our input. We can't control the opportunities life offers us. We can hope for positive encounters, but we will meet callers who attempt to use our lives to support their inappropriate ideas. We'll also run into callers who ask us to compromise ourselves for their benefit. We must adjust our perspective to view life's requests from unbiased positions before we act to ensure we consider the overall impact.

The state of ease the experiment's participants held was challenged as they heard the pain from the student when he was "shocked." Although they had the opportunity to decline to participate in the task prior to that moment, that scream was the instant that displayed the reality of their choice. That was the moment each participant was offered an additional chance to invite a new state of being and back out of the task. They could've refused to continue, and some did. But they also faced the option to accept the new state inspired by the scream and continue the task. Those who continued to deliver shocks ignored the discomfort they felt within, made peace with it, or didn't have a problem with what they were doing. We can't externally identify someone's internal state; we can only observe their actions. If someone isn't aware of their internal activity, they will continue to move through life without this awareness.

We can ignore that the shocks we deliver will be absorbed somewhere in the world, but we can't provide a shock and not expect it to impact life regardless of who ultimately will be held responsible for the act. Therefore, we must discover the relationship between our presence and the impact of our actions. That view offers us a minor glimpse of our impact on life. As we deliver shocks to others, we shouldn't ignore the internal effects of our actions. As we pursue, consume, and accumulate things we consider normal, we should become aware of the impact we are applying on our inner being. There's always an effect within that will eventually cause problems if we neglect it.

We must allow space to recognize the negative influences we encounter that are seeking acceptance. We should always consider the potential for beauty or destruction accompanying our thoughts and actions. We shouldn't only focus on ourselves or our group's interests. If we're here to impact the world, shouldn't we expect that sometimes we have to sacrifice our personal comfort for the betterment of all. Discovering and consciously using awareness plays a significant role in intentionally fulfilling our purpose. It's also our best defense against the opposing influential forces we encounter. This awareness is the tool that allows us to recognize the impact of the ideas and concepts we're bringing to the physical world.

When we observe our surroundings, our inner being interprets what we're experiencing. When we receive that input from the world, we relate it to prior experiences to help us react. Our current state will always be a factor in the way we see what's occurring in that moment. It's predetermining how this event will touch us before we even experience it. That judgment will be a dominant factor as we transition through the experience. The view we're holding could cause unnecessary pain and destruction if we're not using our awareness appropriately. We shouldn't allow prior experiences that we haven't internally settled impact our real-time engagement with life.

I Already Answered

Chapter 15

Global Coverage

We can become comfortable ignoring our contributions in life, but the beliefs we hold become the words and actions that shape our lives. They control what we're willing to accept and attempt to block the things we don't want to experience. We're so entangled in our personal lives and physical assets that we shrug off the atmosphere we're creating and the philosophies we're allowing to dominate our lives through our mindset. That's the same dangerous oversight that allowed issues to develop into local, regional, and global conflicts in the past. Our history has proven that one person can keep a dangerous concept alive, but a vulnerable, distracted, and easily manipulated group can make it thrive.

Although our history lessons focus on the acts that occurred, we must go beyond the actions. We need to uncover the perspectives of those who lived through the experiences. That's the best way to learn and apply the lessons to our current situations. When we study the activities that led to events such as civil unrest, cultural conflicts, and world wars, we must try to understand the circumstances that paved the way for destruction. We have to identify the underlying influences that led to so many people accepting and silently approving of the destructive visions they were offered. That's essential if we wish to prevent similar circumstances in our own lives. The hundreds or thousands of individual lives always energize the activities that move the world. That's where we play our part.

Carrying Concepts

Since birth, we've affected the world through our physical existence. Although we influence life with our actions, we also influence by sustaining our ideas and beliefs. We know that concepts and ideologies can't survive on their own. They're maintained by those who support, uphold, and defend them. The ideas we endorse have a widespread impact on life through our words and actions as we interact with others.

We must ensure the essence we send out is what we genuinely desire to express. Life doesn't forget any of our contributions. Life sustains every idea we deploy when someone accepts it. Life also records the influence we embrace from others. Time moves forward and presents us with the world we've collectively designed through the individual and collective ideals we support. Our presence breathes life into every concept we hold, allowing them to survive.

Some people will use their lives to sustain concepts that wonderfully move the world. Others will promote disruption and confusion. Some will support concepts that breathe beauty. Others will use their inherent ability to create pain and disharmony. Your commitment to the ideas passes them into the next moment, next year, and forever if we continue to sustain them. A concept can't erase from existence until it's spiritually eliminated.

You don't need a neuroscientist or a religious leader to explain this aspect of your existence. You may not understand precisely why you're here, but you can see what is occurring through your presence. You are contributing to the version of the world that currently exists. You are also sculpting the image of what tomorrow will be. You are adding to what will collectively be and removing what we will collectively delete from existence. You'll never discover your contributions if you don't acknowledge your activity.

Everyone is contributing to the essence and spirit of the world. Though physically limited, your existence has a specific effect on the planet. When a group or nation's views on an issue lean in a direction, you are a part of that change. Even when your opinion doesn't agree with the majority, your presence prevents the prevailing stance from moving too far in that opposing direction. Your impact may not appear on the news, but it is present. You don't need a huge platform or branded image to influence life. Your existence sets you in the role of contributing to the world's essence in the present. Your presence offers your idea the possibility of greater relevance in the future, for better or worse.

Conveying Messages

Our physical accomplishments are only symbols that represent our mindset. Our true legacies are the spiritual births and transfers we radiate while we're here and those we pass to the next generations. The concepts you project through your being will live through the people you touch and the ones they touch. This process is continuous. The spiritual effect you present to the world is far more powerful than your physical activity. You can't physically touch everyone but can spiritually touch many through your presence. You could be the most charitable person alive; that won't have a more powerful impact than the spiritual effect you present.

As concepts can't survive in the world without our upkeep, they can't stay in our individual lives without our acceptance. Words don't have any power, but they can be the most potent force on Earth. Ironically, they don't have any life until the receiver breathes life into them through acceptance. We can listen to constructive or destructive words; neither has any hurtful or uplifting effect until we accept them. Similarly, we can listen to affirmations to move us, but they're ineffective until we spiritually accept them. Spiritual acceptance is the act of breathing life into what we receive from others. We always have the choice to accept the words and images we receive or reject them. Once we accept them, they can affect our lives in various ways. If we abandon them, we disable their ability to damage or inspire us. That is one of our essential defenses against the power of influence.

Disruptive Contacts

Acknowledging your essence is vital to understanding the issues occurring in your personal life and in the world. We neglect our well-being when we don't tie the impact of our nonphysical activities to the results we experience in life. When we fall short of a goal, we look at all the concrete evidence explaining why we didn't complete our objective. We've learned to use the acronym 'SMART' (Specific, Measurable, Achievable, Realistic, and Timely) when we set goals. But even when we follow this guidance, we may not find success when we're under the burden of our physical lives. We can look at the steps we didn't complete and the time we didn't commit to our goal; what we fail to emphasize are the formless aspects existing behind our efforts.

We're constantly approached by influences that affect us. These forces might not have anything to do with our personal lives, yet they have an impact. When we can't find the connection to the influences that derail us, we continue to allow things that we can't see to affect our journey negatively. We can't elevate beyond our current circumstances following that guidance. We must learn to identify the hidden forces before inadvertently accepting their undesired effects.

The therapy sessions we attend, the inspirational words we hear, and the life-changing events we witness are only effective if we spiritually accept them. That means we go beyond simply stating a commitment. It becomes a part of us. The difference between someone who transforms their life and one who remains tied to the past is their internal action. They either accept, deny, or reject the inspiration that life offers. That's an effect you can't measure externally, but it's something you can examine within yourself.

We must look within as often as possible to discover the concepts and beliefs we are fostering. Viewing the world around us will show us exactly what we are embracing. Ideas can't survive without human support, and they can't endure without our acceptance. We were born to animate the world by establishing and sustaining concepts through our existence. We must use our spiritual awareness to discover the ideas we're supporting from within.

Many of our biggest undertakings approach in a physical form, but they attack us internally. Your ability to manage life's difficulties and disruptions determines your well-being. When you spiritually mismanage situations, the results are always displayed in your life. You may not recognize the origin because you aren't observing your life spiritually. You aren't looking at how your internal reactions destroy or uplift you. Discovering the source of your activities and the source of your influences is at the root of spirituality. You must be able to tie your actions to their internal origins.

I Already Answered

Part Four

Premium Alternatives

Chapter 16

Goals, Calls, & Self-discovery

When you're in a contest, the results tell you how well you performed. In life, there isn't an observable finish line. You'll never reach a set destination or achieve a particular feat and claim that you won the game of life. That should be a natural indication that life is not a competition. But there are siblings, friends, coworkers, classmates, and others that we're measured against. That may be considered normal, but there's nothing natural or healthy about it. It creates psychological problems that often surface from our improper, unethical, and irresponsible behavior from desperate attempts to "win."

The only measurement we need throughout life is computed within ourselves. We need to be able to determine if we're growing, stuck in a cycle, or falling into depression. That's never a comparison against others. It's an objective look at our well-being. We need to partner with life to take an unbiased look at how we're answering life's calls. An excellent opportunity to view our growth, expansion, or decline is by setting goals and observing our approach, mindset, and transition along the journey.

Personal Measurements

Although we typically think of goals as a means to accomplishing objectives, we should also use them for the self-discovery they can provide. Setting goals, defining objectives, and making plans are key tools in observing our internal activity. Using our awareness, we can identify connections between our approaches to situations, the essence and moods we present, and our results. And maybe more importantly, goals can help us identify our true intentions. Although the goal is important, wisdom comes from observing our inner and external activity as we pursue our objectives. Setting goals and observing our activities as we pursue them is vital to personal development and increasing our self-awareness.

When we set goals, we decide to challenge our present comfort. The goal we've set is our acceptance of the challenge, but life promises to test our determination. When we get into the steps, it can become difficult to sustain our commitment. Callers always approach with fascinating and attractive proposals that can woo or seduce us. We have to decide to keep pressing forward or allow the beauty of completing our goal to be overshadowed by the allure of something different. Random calls can cancel the beauty we see in the goals and objectives we need to pursue. Although the distractions may be physical, the attraction isn't. It's a more potent force than your desire to accomplish your goal. You can lock yourself away from what's distracting you, but you can't physically eliminate the attraction because it attacks your spirit.

If you can't stick to the path leading to your objective, you need to discover what's actually preventing your progress. The answer is something hidden behind the activities you engage in every day. There's beauty all around that conflicts with the direction we want to travel. We can choose to pursue the beauty we encounter or stick to our objective. If the attraction to any distraction exceeds our bond to our goal, we'll follow the new beauty and abandon our intention, even if the beauty is harmful or detrimental.

Our inner activity is more robust than any self-improvement habit or physical defense we attempt to install. This inner activity can easily allow you to pursue something that's mentally or physically hurting you. We see it when we study the effects of drug abuse and addiction, but the same activity is occurring in all our lives. It's easy to target the habits society considers harmful, but anything that hinders your well-being is destructive. An addiction to running your business could conflict with your need to exercise as you've been directed by your doctor. Just because the habit you're performing is considered favorable to the external world doesn't mean it isn't hazardous to your life.

Physical defenses don't work without personal input. Inner alignment is the only force that keeps you in sync with your intention. It's true in relationships, commitments to employment, educational pursuits, and every other goal. Your attraction to other things isn't wrong, but not knowing when they divert you is devastating. When you aren't aware of their presence, the damage they cause isn't apparent. You may recognize some of the effects in your life, but the real damage they inflict is the spiritual misdirection they present. You may believe you're focused on your goal, but distractions spiritually move you to other areas. This misdirection is always a factor in the agreements we make with ourselves.

Self-Intervention

Research, data, and surveys are invaluable tools and are critical to providing information to society. Unfortunately, our reliance on these tools can unintentionally negatively influence our awareness. When research shows a slim chance of success at an objective, we might allow that data to negatively affect our approach. Instead of using the data to inform us of the challenge, we allow the information to subdue our effort and commitment from the beginning of our journey. As we move through the steps involved in accomplishing our goals, we allow the data to drive our results. If we were observant, we would find our effort aligned with the average results the data presented.

If statistics show that fifty percent of marriages end in divorce, that can impact your mindset. That number can influence your commitment and effort in the marriage because the percentage states that the average marriage is headed for divorce anyway. You may be operating with the mindset that divorce is typical and expected. If you're not present and aware, you won't see yourself internally relying on that data and allowing it to influence your life.

The problem with totally relying on general statistics is that the data you're using is never personal. The information offers a broad, helpful view, but we might use it detrimentally. Instead of building strength and courage for the journey ahead, we use it to internally justify our commitment deficit. Instead of viewing the percentages that prove the possibility of success, we move based on the probability of failure. Regardless of how we view the statistics, we need to remember that the numbers we're looking at don't identify an individual. The numbers are representative of a group. It doesn't state that you will fail because the group tended to struggle with this task. You have to tell yourself that the statistics aren't personal consciously.

If you want to buy into the "average" that many studies prove, that's your choice. You can continue to accept negative statistics and allow them to affect you, or you can choose to answer your calls with clarity. If you desire to exceed your present conditions, you must become the one who represents the slim chance at success. When studies show how difficult it is to change habits, you can become one of the few to find success. When they state that ninety percent of New Year's resolutions are abandoned, you can be in the ten percent that succeed. When the research claims that the average person can't do something, you can complete it.

Excelling Beyond Calls

To exceed the average, we must set ourselves up for success from the onset. We start by rejecting anything that suggests we'll be mediocre. We have to establish the environment for success that we'll feed off. That's how we become the exception who succeeds against the odds. It doesn't matter how big or small our goal is. We must reject the attitude of accepting the average. That is our spiritual choice. The opportunity to succeed or fail is within the individual who attempts the task. The vital step is to reduce the belief in average. Let others fill the ranks of the ordinary; you don't have to be one of them.

The individual matters more than the data. Every unique problem requires a different approach to resolve. Our lives are unique and require personal investigation that surpasses general research. Failing to pursue a desire because the research doesn't look promising could be a huge mistake. You have to decide that embracing average isn't acceptable.

If we don't understand our inner impact on our results, then the research reflects the facts. Most of us won't succeed at that objective. But is the data that confirms the high failure rate influencing your effort? The reason behind the numbers is the vital information we can't access because we can't speak to everyone included in the study. But you can determine why you give one hundred percent, fifty percent, or ten percent in any area of your life. Then, you can address your issues and move forward with a new level of awareness even if you can't resolve the issue.

Outsiders are playing a guessing game when they are viewing your life. No one can see the internal influences that are impacting you. Although many of the challenges we face are similar, there aren't any cut-and-paste actions to apply because we're all unique. Our family members, friends, and teachers are using their own experiences and knowledge. Unfortunately, none of that gives them a clear view of our circumstances from within. Their advice comes from their perspective, even when they attempt to be empathetic.

Experts studying human behavior have documented the similarities in our situations but haven't produced a universal solution that applies to everyone. We're all having unique experiences. So, we must do the work even when others are trying to help us.

We may have the best therapist on the planet, but we still have to contribute to our healing. The therapist will equip us with tools and strategies; however, we must apply them daily. For most people, that task is more complicated than recovering from physical ailments. That requires conscious cooperation, which may not be needed for physical healing. After medical intervention, the body can recover from many conditions. Unfortunately, the mind can't heal itself because of our constant meddling and the overflow of influence we allow to intervene.

When we walk away from a therapy session or put down the self-help book, we return to the world we knew before the encounter. Guidance from others can be helpful, but we must put in the work. We have to live our lives. That's why your involvement is necessary to receive the healing we seek. We must invest ourselves in our recovery. We can learn a tremendous amount about ourselves as we move through the goals and objectives we set.

Chapter 17

Authentic Expectancy

We assume we set our eyes on the best situation for ourselves, but often that isn't true. Instead, we put our faith in what we believe we can accomplish or what we've been sold to desire, neither of which may be best for our wellness. Our belief in that vision will guide our effort. It also determines the energy and importance we assign to the things we deal with. Our belief is a force that propels or subdues our internal commitment. That essence reflects in our attitude, enthusiasm, effort, and feelings about any subject. If we don't check the source of our belief in the things we want, we'll pursue them based on what callers have provided rather than our authentic aspirations.

When we work toward our goals, our results reveal our inner commitment and true intentions. If our accomplishment matches our initial goal, we feel we succeeded. But even when we don't achieve our stated objective, we likely still met our *actual* target. Our true intention is the authentic agreement we established within. Our intentions are only moving us based on our sincere intent, not the vague, unrealistic goals we set. We won't fully support those verbal goals unless true intentions back them up. We can deceive ourselves by appearing to commit to our lofty goals, but in reality, we're moving towards the lesser outcome we trust.

Disruptive Shortcuts

If the materialization of our effort doesn't match our expectations, we must determine where we fell short to learn from it. Sometimes external circumstances might prevent us from accomplishing our goals, but we shouldn't automatically look for shallow excuses before we look within. We achieve what we honestly believe. We must recognize that we have the most influence on anything we encounter.

It's equally important to see that we can surrender that influence to others without realizing we've given it away. We can allow words and opinions to degrade our internal image, affecting our intent. Based on that inferior image, we may abandon our chance at victory before the physical journey begins. No one can tell us when this occurs because it's an internal activity we must discover ourselves. The words could have been spoken years prior, but their effect could be lingering in our lives.

Our results can also reveal the quality of the effort we used in an activity. Looking back at our results is a form of reverse engineering that ensures we learn from our experiences. It's an excellent way for us to quantify our spiritual input and commitment after the fact. Although viewing external events is essential, complete wisdom ensures we review the inner activity that drove our actions. Only you know the energy and effort you put into the activity. You know what your commitment was and when you let things disrupt it. Those aspects tell us exactly how we impacted our results.

Our actions display the physical effort we apply towards results, but we must determine the inner agreements that led to our movements. The effort we provide can be amplified or diminished by our spirit. That's the spiritual effect we have over the things we encounter. Anything can affect that essence, so we need to acknowledge its existence. We can always intensify our impact through our internal commitment to a particular area. That begins with our initial intention.

We must acknowledge spirituality as the essence we currently present to everything in life. Everyone offers their nature to the things they encounter based on their beliefs. We must see the aspects of spirituality that connect our inner presence to the physical experiences we have every day. Simple awareness of our spiritual influence on our lives is an understanding that will increase our well-being.

We use phrases such as "Get back up again!" and "When the going gets tough, the tough get going!" which target our spirit. They're not intellectual. If you don't have true awareness, the sayings won't move you. They're just empty words of encouragement. If the words do spark inspiration, they'll only move you to your preexisting intent. You likely won't surpass your prearranged level even though you could.

Nonphysical Effort

We may not recognize the inner transitions we experience because they don't require our conscious acknowledgment. Everything we accomplish comes through our spiritual presence. If we start our journey with doubt and skepticism, that will feed our effort. Our results will likely meet our initial intent unless we allow it to change. We can't have a successful life transformation without an altered spirit. The change will only be temporary when we attempt to move without a spiritual transition. We'll continue to struggle until a shift breaks through.

When we build a relationship with our spiritual presence, we can create a new understanding of life. We find that the situations we experience today don't have to affect us in the same way tonight, tomorrow, or beyond. We can create a perspective that acknowledges but downgrades any harmful elements.

We can work towards a better scenario without trying to bypass today. We can allow the factors we can't alter to be, while believing in ourselves to do the things we can. This is how we act in the present to bring about a new tomorrow. We can build up our faith by doing the things today that will lead to that beauty, but never at the expense of today. We must learn to spiritually transition through the present to move forward.

Our current situation might appear to cause our frustration, but we must allow today to be as it is. If we could change today to be what we want it to be, we would have done it. Since we can't force today to be different, we must allow it to exist. Callers may approach and attempt to return your spiritual focus to the negative aspects of the present, but you can allow things to exist without attaching to the disturbing qualities. We must learn to let unchanging people be who they are. We also must allow things that we can't immediately change to exist. However, we can spiritually alter our acceptance so we can press forward without allowing it to damage our presence.

We must allow some things to occur because we don't have ultimate control over everything in life. We can eliminate things, turn away from individuals, and dodge scenarios, but we can't circumvent life. There are aspects of our lives we can't divorce. We need to become aware of the concept of allowing versus accepting. Acceptance can cause what we're receiving to affect other areas of life. When we allow things, we let that situation stand as it is without letting it influence our thoughts, behavior, or actions. It's a minor difference in definition but a dynamic difference in practice.

If we know someone unreliable, we shouldn't trust that they'll do what they say. We should allow them to be unreliable without harming ourselves. If we find ourselves depending on that person, we've let their unreliability affect our lives. Instead, we should allow them to be unreliable without letting it alter our being. We can still love that person and allow them to be as they are without altering our being.

Many things that occur within your world will remain outside of your physical control. Awareness is vital to allowing these aspects to exist without causing mental and emotional problems that disturb your state of being. You can allow things to exist without impacting your spirit. That impact can disturb your ability to see life through an impartial lens.

Chapter 18

Effort or Alignment

Life always offers us the path of least resistance.

But it also provides alternative paths that callers bring.

It's up to us to align with the path that leads to desirable ends, or we'll struggle with the available alternative routes when someone calls.

When we think of the least possible resistance, we think of physical obstructions. We think about the physical obstacles that stand between us and our goals. If I want to lose ten pounds, I consider the change in diet and exercise that might lead me to my goal. But those are only the physical aspects I will encounter to accomplish my goal. If I don't convert myself into someone who knows I can lose ten pounds, I'll struggle to perform the required steps.

The path of least resistance can't be physical if something presides over your physical effort. That must be the path of least resistance. That's your inner being. You'll find that you can begin to lose weight by making adjustments that don't require extensive exercise. The same effect exists in every aspect of life. If you look internally before your actions, you'll find immaterial answers that affect your physical effort.

Internal Agreements

We try to align with the right path by setting goals and creating plans that point us in the right direction. But first, we need to create an internal agreement that aligns with our objective. Your journey through life is dominated by the agreements offering the least resistance. Those are the aspects you comfortably align with.

If you desire to further your education and spend more time socializing, the one that offers the least resistance will dominate. There's space for both to occur, but we have to create the opportunity for them to occur simultaneously. If we find less resistance in another area, we will likely follow that other path instead. If you make tangible changes without applying an interior conversion, you're setting yourself up for a long, unnecessary struggle.

If you want a promotion in your career, don't wait until a position opens to start showing you want it. First, you internally prepare yourself as an indispensable asset in the present moment. Then, that internal adjustment will manifest into actions that display your dedication. When the promotion opportunity appears, you'll be the natural selection. But that doesn't mean you will automatically receive the promotion. It only proves to you and anyone observant that you deserve it.

Your awareness will also display what you should or shouldn't try to stay aligned with when your effort isn't recognized or respected. In other words, it may be time to move on when you know you've committed to your craft and fail to receive the recognition that should accompany your effort. But, if you know you didn't commit as you should have, you shouldn't be falsely upset.

Prearranged Development

During clinical trials, the medical community uncovered a phenomenon known as the Placebo effect. While researching a drug's effectiveness, they observed improvements in some patients who received simulated drugs known as placebos. The patients believed they were receiving treatment from the medication, but these placebos didn't contain ingredients that provided relief. Instead, it made the patients believe they received medication to improve their situation. These trials allowed researchers to evaluate the effectiveness of the medicine given to other patients compared to the placebo. However, the results documented some placebo patients had changes in pain, heart rate, and other activity. This discovery prompted further studies into this phenomenon.

These results display an ability to experience benefits through internal activity. The belief in treatment sparked a positive change in the individual. Some might argue that reducing pain doesn't prove a change, yet it is real for those who experience it. The placebo effect is now an inseparable factor in modern medical research.

Rearranging our perception of circumstances can spark a positive change. This discovery emphasized the importance of the total care experience for hospital patients. The patient's confidence in the administered care appears to be a factor in their outcome. The inner acceptance of a positive experience can trigger improvements that may not be measurable but exist. A simulated drug, a caring nursing staff, or a concerned physician can inspire that confidence. The power is in the positive acceptance by the patient.

We shouldn't neglect the opposite effect of this phenomenon. If a positive inner acceptance can enhance a situation, negative acceptance can result in unfavorable results. For example, when a patient feels care is lacking or they believe the facilities are substandard, that outlook can affect their wellness. Could that be true in underserved communities which lack modern facilities and have limited medical personnel? When statistics show an imbalance in these communities, can the feeling from the environment be a negative contributor that's immeasurable?

The placebo effect reinforces the importance of elevating your awareness above your physical situation. Can you prove the activity of the placebo effect or any activity occurring within? The only person that you can prove it to is yourself. When you do, you understand the benefit of knowing that your approach to anything will enormously affect the outcome. You don't need others to believe in the awareness that works for you. You only need to be able to tap into it to help you along in your journey. We should all investigate whether a nonphysical effort can produce a positive (or negative) effect. That suggests that I can enhance my results by altering the internal views that I own. For example, if I have a goal, I can internally create an environment that can aid in achieving that goal. Alternatively, I may produce a climate that guarantees I will never succeed.

The effect is personal, and one person's results won't match others. It's not what the activity does to you; it's the internal environment you create while taking action that enhances or degrades your results. Our ability to internally manipulate our outlook can tremendously affect the results we achieve. The human spirit is powerful when led from within. But it's also a powerful force when led by external influence. Understanding this, we must acknowledge the powerful impact that our environmental effects have on us. We must take ownership to ensure we lead ourselves in a desirable direction.

If you don't accept that you are the dominant factor in your successes and failures, you won't surpass your current position in life. You must be willing to move forward with a new approach. You have to consider your intangible influence on your situation. When you recognize that you are the most important factor in your joy, satisfaction, and content, you have identified the enemy of your success. But we must remember that tremendous influences can steal that power and make it their own. We must learn to lead from within as we maneuver through our circumstances.

Adjusting Your Settings

How many family disruptions and failed relationships do we have to experience before we decide to look in the mirror? Instead of looking within, we blame the other person's shortcomings as the problem in our relationships. We choose to focus on the flaws in our partner rather than look at our contributions. Indeed, the other person has issues, but we aren't perfect either. When we finally decide to look at ourselves, we mistakenly look at the physical aspects we bring to relationships. The image reflected in the mirror only shows your physical qualities. The part that's guiding your life exists beneath the surface. It's leading you to success, failure, joy, frustration, and everything else. That's the part you must become intimately familiar with.

A closer look might reveal that relationships expose qualities within us that we've chosen to brush off. We sometimes focus so much on the imperfections of others that we overlook our contributions. How many days of frustration must we endure before we stop trying to force changes in others without acknowledging our negative input? When we alter our approach to circumstances, things instantly adjust from our renewed perspective. When we discover shortcomings in ourselves, we shouldn't beat ourselves up. We have to build our self-awareness so we learn as much as possible. That knowledge sparks the end of self-created confusion in relationships and other interactions. It is a part of the most valuable information you can learn.

The constant flow of activity from life becomes a distraction preventing us from using our natural ability to deal with the issues we face. Interruptions cause us to misinterpret, misunderstand, and improperly hold perspectives that could harm instead of improving a situation. We then find ourselves relying on that unfavorable outlook and we disregard the alternative perspectives that could help.

Ancient teachings emphasized the importance of acknowledging our inner guidance, yet we continue to deny it by focusing on the physical obstructions. The calls we receive move our attention further away from maximizing our creativity. That causes us to misuse our inner strength and the assistance it could provide.

Quiet Strength

Our essence moves us towards our goals or pushes them away. It's always a factor in directing our lives. When we have an optimistic feeling about something, that mood causes us to take committed actions. When we look at our spiritual outlook towards things, we can determine what physical measures we've put in motion to obtain it. We also can see what's preventing us from reaching our objectives.

Getting into the spirit is the perfect phrase to describe the feeling of internal activity. It's the act of getting into the mood of being something and sustaining it. Again, we can use the example of feeling nervous before we give a speech. Eventually, we have to put the nerves aside and get into the mood of going out there to do it. That's getting into the spirit. We move past what we currently feel about a situation and create a more agreeable perspective. If we remain in a nervous, fearful state, it will display in the speech. That will manifest from our inability to advance from the negative state.

When we value something in life, we must not view it in a negative state. A concept in practice called 'Fake it till you make it' encourages us to act as if we've already obtained what we desire. In truth, it requires minimal physical activity. Instead, it compels us to visualize and exercise our desire mentally. The faking is not intended for the external world; the faking is for you. The faking is to solidify the vision you have for yourself before you begin to act.

When we fake it in the external world, it always comes crashing down on us if we can't perform. Acting before we solidify confidence can lead to failure. In society, when we pretend to be something that we aren't, we can be prosecuted for false impersonation. Taking on a role in life before internally accepting it can also lead to internal strife. As a result, we won't experience the success we're trying to achieve.

You can't successfully become a firefighter without the required knowledge and training. But, even with those assets in-hand, you remain a danger to yourself and others if you don't have the inner assurance to perform the tasks. Even though you've never fought a fire, you must begin to feel yourself into the role. During your training, you'll be pushed to experience the feeling of the actual event. If you have not internally transitioned during your training and preparations, it will display in your actions during the field exercises. Recognizing your inability to transition will show you and your instructors that you're not ready to move forward.

Education and training are vital, but it takes something more to be successful at anything. We have to internally move our spirit. Once we spiritually accept the new vision and eliminate our previous outlook, physical activities can begin. We must spiritually operate from the emerging state we've established to start seeing the effects when callers approach. Working from the old state will continue to produce old results. If we aren't leading from the new state, we'll return to what we've previously established. Then we'll continue to see the old state reappear in our world based on our activities.

When we spiritually uplift ourselves to see life from the new state, we can transition in that direction. If we continue to act from our current state, we won't transform. The faking that we perform is never for the external world. The faking is always for you. You begin to see yourself in the desired state instead of continuing to see what today offers as the only possibility. The faking internally lifts you towards the new state. It occupies your mind and begins to lead your actions. Manifestations always follow your inner activity.

The Force that Moves

Have you ever wanted to neglect an activity but forced yourself into the mood to do it? That's a force that can't be measured, but it exists. Regardless of the pressure you felt from an approaching deadline, the bottom line is that nothing forced you into action. You've had deadlines before that you blew off. You could easily blow off anything you desire to. Something gets you into the mood to accomplish things when you get into the right spirit.

Acknowledging the reality of this force allows us to use it when we need it. These inner activities drive the physical acts we perform. Unfortunately, they also fuel the actions we fail to deliver. They prevent us from physically moving in the direction that we say we desire to go.

Discovering something within ourselves that is preventing us from moving toward a goal becomes game-changing wisdom. We've identified something that is causing frustration in our lives. Even if we don't take any other action with the information, we now understand something that's been causing frustration. Knowing it's acting within us can make an enormous difference in our world.

Seeing this activity is enlightening; however, controlling it is where the power to create our world exists. When we understand the driving force behind our physical actions, we can determine why we move in the directions we're moving in. When we gain control of it, we can start to move the self-constructed boundaries that formerly prevented us from achieving our desires. That will help us decide when we need to answer calls and when we need to press decline.

Refresh

We can take the lead in controlling our activity from within, but we can't ignore our reliance on the physical aspects of life. It's been our primary guide through our physical senses and the scientific proof that we collectively verify. Therefore, to relate to this inner activity, we might need to attempt to sense it spatially. That's where activities such as yoga, meditation, and creative visualization are helpful. Many people use these activities to touch their inner being purposely. Connecting these practices to our daily lives is the essential step when we participate in them.

When we walk away from our spiritual exercise, we need to retain the essence. That inner activity we sense in our practice places us in touch with the presence that is always available. We need to be able to use it as a tool instead of relying on deceptive practices we've learned and adopted throughout our journeys. The feeling we sense in our wellness practice is always available to inspire responses that can manifest as positive answers to any call or situation. But if we walk away from our spiritual practice and leave what we touched behind, it won't be available when we react to life. We shouldn't struggle to remain focused because that leads to frustration.

We shouldn't participate in wellness practices insincerely. That could lead to a self-righteous state that will be difficult to recognize and recover from. We risk falling into this state when we follow trends. Our belief in the insincere practice we're exercising might seem remarkable, but the false condition is only temporarily satisfying. Your interactions in the world display reality, but you may be ignoring it because you're too entrenched in the belief of your practice. Awareness surrounds you in truth and delivers you from faulty beliefs that ignore your true impact on reality.

Access to Your Network

Sometimes, you know you need to take action in your life, but you don't allow yourself to move. The beauty of recognizing true spirituality is that it encourages you to proceed with awareness while you approach that fear. It pushes you away from unhealthy circumstances because you recognize them through your presence. When you encounter adverse situations, you won't be inspired to cause further harm. Instead, awareness encourages you to move confidently in times of despair. You address these situations from within and don't allow the role or the scenario to direct you. You ensure your controlled inner activity moves you.

If we desire to alter the person we present to the world, we must go all out and take on the role. People who transform themselves get into the spirit of what they want to be and become it. They don't take on the part in the morning, abandon it by lunch, and then get back into character after dinner. Instead, they become who they need to be.

When you see a friend at work, you might put on the role you want to display in front of them. You may be successful in fooling them, but that doesn't matter. Deceiving your friends, parents, partner, and anyone else doesn't matter. The only one that matters in becoming the new person is you. You can deceive everyone into believing you are something you want them to think you are, and you may be successful. It happens all the time. But you shouldn't try to deceive yourself. Even when you try to fake it till you make it, you're not fooling yourself. You are elevating yourself. You must spiritually embrace the nature of the person you want to be and live it to the max. But at the same time, you must maintain your presence to observe yourself in the role without becoming spiritually consumed by it. That's when the characteristics carry over to affect other areas negatively.

What is Love?

Internal alignment is the path of least resistance and is the simplest way to achieve any goal. Unfortunately, this alignment is easily disturbed when callers approach with alternatives. You can't truly begin to transition from your old state of being into a new one until you make an internal adjustment. You must fall out of love with the old ways and embrace the new ones. Your new agreement must overtake your previously established state.

Inner alignment is an example of love, but it's not infatuation. It's love in its purest, most sincere, and genuine form. No tricks, no deception, no attempting to achieve something with a secondary aim in mind. True spirituality is the natural act of getting into the spirit of your objective. It's falling in love with that idea. It's the ability to take on the role of what you want to be and naturally do the things necessary to bring it to reality. It's not scheming and plotting to get what you want. When life sends callers to disrupt, your love for your objective won't allow it.

Spirituality is the path of least resistance within you. You stop fighting the things you have to do to become the person you want to become. You stop avoiding the activities that will lead you to success. You naturally accept the responsibility that comes with fulfilling the role of your desire. Exercising won't be a burden because you'll creatively find a way to incorporate it into your life. You can't feel like it's a burden because that would cause resistance. Any resistance can lead to alternative actions.

If you have a demanding dream, you won't let family, friends, or fear redirect your desire. Instead, you follow through with the work required of someone who genuinely wants that dream to materialize. If you find yourself struggling to commit to the required activities, then maybe the criticism from your friends and family is justifiable. Then, the fear you are experiencing is warranted.

The lack of devotion to your dream is apparent to them. They're trying to get you to see that your dedication isn't where it needs to be to reach the success you claim to desire. When you view their criticism from a spiritual perspective, you may see their honest intentions. That should trigger you to confront your loyalty to your desire honestly. You can't afford to risk everything without a spiritual commitment that matches or exceeds the physical requirements.

We may not like the message someone relays to us, but we must look within to determine the validity of the message. We should never shoot the messenger. Instead, their message should touch you spiritually. That interaction may cause you to recommit to your desire, or it may cause you to face the inner truth that you may be displaying to the world. There's no shame in rejecting a desire you're not spiritually engaged to. The shame is in pursuing something you're not truly committed to.

On Track

When you're spiritually aligned, you won't return to the old state of being you left behind when adversity approaches. You'll be comfortable dealing with life in the new state. If you aspire to be a leader in a group, you won't fade into the background when it's time to lead. You'll step up to meet the challenge and see it through until it's resolved. That's proof that you have accepted that new role in your life.

We always answer the question of who we are by our reactions to the present moment. If you continue to react to things as you did in the past, you haven't made the transition. On the other hand, when you notice a difference in your natural reaction to situations, you know you're on your way to solidifying the desired change. We don't need someone to tell us we've changed; we must be aware. Then we will know we've made our transition to the new state or that we haven't. Spirituality is the path to every transformation, even when it's an undesirable change.

When we decide to take a new approach to life, we expose ourselves to the residual influences that come with that new vision. Many of those factors will approach without warning. We must maintain our awareness as we transition into any new status. We can easily sacrifice our balanced awareness to adopt a damaging presence in route to our vision. Our desire for success can lead us to obtain our dreams, but it can also lead us down a path that introduces us to undesirable circumstances that we never intended to face. You can look throughout society to find examples of financial or material success with limited respect for life and humanity that might accompany it. Our awareness always offers a view of our position on every issue, but we can easily ignore it as we pursue our desires.

Premium Alternatives

Chapter 19

Attachments

Is there any relationship between your approach to the situations you face and your results?

Do your mood, attitude, and demeanor affect your circumstances? If so, how much?

Every event in our day offers the opportunity to sink or swim in that area of life. Until we acknowledge that fact, we'll remain stuck in our predicaments. Being stuck is not necessarily negative. You could be stuck in a positive place where you are thriving. But you're likely stuck in a negative pattern. That's when the mountain that represents your problem can't be moved.

You may not be able to move the mountain, but there are plenty of other methods to confront it if you look for them. The clutter of life isn't allowing you to recognize the solution. When you use your creativity with your awareness, you can find alternatives. You may also find the prosperous relationships that have been eluding you. You'll discover how to climb any mountain impeding your growth or learn to adjust to it as you continue moving forward.

You can't physically control everything that happens. Even though you can remove physical obstructions that keep you attached to your current circumstances, others can easily replace them. Therefore, discovering the things that spiritually link you to obstacles is critical. Identifying your attachments, which can prevent your progress, will determine the elements needing adjustment or release.

Attachments are the root details that internally move us. We may not consciously acknowledge their presence, but they are participants in directing our lives. They include the concepts we've accepted without acknowledging them, the knowledge we've accumulated and refuse to challenge, and the beliefs we passionately hold. They are immaterial. They live in our being. Unfortunately, we rarely address these aspects of transformation when trying to improve.

Attachments are the specific points that bind us to our current activities. They're the answers when we can't determine why we're struggling to quit an unwanted habit. They're the unseen factors binding us below the surface of the behavior. Some people can stop destructive habits cold turkey. What we observe from the outside is the end of their behavior, but the transition required an internal adjustment that resulted in the change. That internal adjustment causes the change to become a reality. An epiphany or fear may have sparked it, but the ability to harness and utilize that level of control can have a powerful effect on your life. That experience can be an excellent opportunity for growth when we understand the internal activity that occurred.

The Effortless Way

When we're struggling to improve who we are and neglecting things that could enhance our well-being, it can be hard to identify the problem. Something is freezing us in our current state of being and won't allow us to break through. When we know we need to transform a part of our being, the effortless way is the right way. The effortless way refers to the inner activity that makes our responses seem automatic. Though our response seems involuntary, we've previously established a view we run to without hesitation. We rely on that perspective when responding to life's calls. When we need to change something in our lives, we should start by acknowledging our current understanding of our situation. We especially need to discover those automatic responses we're relying on in our lives.

The effortless way is the desired relationship between your mindset and your actions when you need to make changes. You need the steps to complete your goals to become second nature. That occurs when there's little to no conflict between your mind and the actions that you have to perform. The closer your goals align with your convictions, the less resistance your mind will create toward the required steps.

When we have distressing thoughts and feelings toward our actions, it creates inner opposition that disrupts our ease. Any belief or thought related to the steps we need to take can affect our progress. Something that we're taught, a point of view we've accepted, or a concept of ourselves we've embraced establishes these ideas within. If our beliefs, principles, or inner agreements disagree with the steps we need to take, we'll introduce disruptions that block our desired change. That creates internal roadblocks that prevent us from completing steps. That opposition requires extra effort to complete the steps and stay aligned with our objective, or we'll give up.

Clarifying Discomfort

In the past, we may have accepted a negative belief that doesn't align with a new opportunity we desire to experience. To move forward with the opportunity, the steps could introduce actions that challenge our current beliefs. That negative thought impacts our self-concept and creates resistance that occurs before we move a muscle. It forces us to make a critical decision. We have to decide to face the discomfort or give up. In most cases, we spiritually surrender long before we physically give up, but we don't see it in real-time. We'll never create a fertile environment to ensure we embrace new actions if we don't confront our inner convictions.

The effortless way requires us to investigate internal obstacles preventing us from improving our lives. These blocks appear as troublesome thoughts and emotions which create resistance by attacking our spirit. You may find that you're unable to overcome that conviction. But at least you know what's preventing you instead of living with the frustration of being stuck.

Completing the steps will require extra effort. Unfortunately, when some callers discover our struggle, they understand that our desire to succeed is one of the best opportunities to exploit us. When we're on a quest to better ourselves, they know we're searching for any advantage to make our transition faster, more accessible, and more manageable. As a result, these callers will approach us with opportunities to help us achieve our objectives with their assistance.

Some of their offers could help us achieve our goals, but none are required. We can purchase a gym membership, a new treadmill, or find a personal trainer to reach our fitness goals, but they aren't needed. They can make it more accessible, but that's because we haven't internally committed to the steps. We're trying to sell it to ourselves by making it more convenient. We haven't prioritized it in our spiritual lives, so we purchase physical items to solidify our commitment.

These props give us something tangible to grasp and moderate the inner turmoil we're experiencing. We're attempting to supplement our limited spiritual commitment to our goal. When spiritually invested, there won't be inconveniences that prevent us from taking the needed steps. We won't need any props to help us commit. Just as nothing can separate us from the bad habits we're already in relationships with until we spiritually divorce them.

Nefarious Callers

Besides the average caller whose services could help us, there's a different type of caller who goes further than offering products, services, or advice. When we're too eager to pursue our desire or unwilling to approach our mindset, we might consider other ways to reach our objectives. That's when opportunistic callers come into play. These callers have the power to advance us on our journey, and they use that authority to see how far we're willing to go. They ask us to perform criminal, sexual, and immoral acts in exchange for their favor. Giving in to their demands offers a high probability of success but comes with a steep price. Their requests exceed the average inner conflict we face because they ask us to compromise our morals and ethics.

If we feel pressured to abandon our integrity or ethics in any way, we're paying a price that always exceeds anything we gain. Every moral or ethical belief we own is a deeply rooted attachment, not simply a common belief. When our thoughts challenge these ideals, we invite an unsettling feeling in the soul. However, when we act against these accepted principles, we create a void within our being by deserting our values. That void won't easily disappear. The internal turmoil created by this void is a fertile environment for a new, dangerous perspective to grow.

The punishment for acting against our moral and ethical codes is severe. When we cross a moral or ethical standard that we elected to live by, we should expect the fallout to be more personal than breaking a law that's externally imposed upon us. A lawyer can help you out of legal issues but cannot rescue you from your ethics. The fallout from your ethical misdeed could have a long-term impact on your presence and state of mind.

Although you may physically achieve your goal in these situations, you also gain a heavy burden attached to it. You want to believe there isn't any fallout from your action, but the impact will live in your conscious and subconscious presence. That impact will present inner disturbances stemming from your actions but will be challenging to see because it won't appear related to your problems.

An option to ease the discomfort from that void is filling it with more activity. Unfortunately, one of the easiest and unnaturally rewarding ways to fill it is to continue the immoral act and settle into this new practice. It's become a more acceptable option because we were rewarded the first time, and we have a similar expectation. Once we cross our moral code without sustaining any apparent damage, it's easier to cross it again.

Tempered Enthusiasm

When we're trying to accomplish a goal, we have to be cautious in our pursuit. Our ambition makes us easy targets for unethical callers who present themselves as allies but only seek to fulfill their selfish desires. When striving to be better or do something we've been unable to do before, we have to move with a clear perspective. Although we should be prepared to face challenges, we shouldn't need to compromise our integrity in any way to achieve our objective. We should expect to make sacrifices to reach our goals, but they should never require us to compromise our ethics and morals.

When we choose to pay for success with our integrity, we aren't using the effortless way to succeed. Instead, we're cutting out the mental and physical effort we should expend in exchange for internal strife that will torment our being. We're taking a costly shortcut. We need to retreat from actions and reevaluate our situation. Unfortunately, the caller will pressure you to make a hasty decision because taking your time to evaluate will likely lead you to reject the offer. The uneasy feeling occurring within yourself in that moment is a warning that must not be glossed over.

It would be best if you walked away from that temptation. The person or situation presenting that opportunity is leading you into spiritual disorder. That occurs when we cross our moral and ethical standards. No one external might punish you for your actions, even if it's illegal. But the discomfort and unease that occur within can be devastating. You'll feel hesitant to vocalize your situation to others because of the embarrassing, improper, and possibly illegal nature. You may also feel compelled to stay quiet to avert damage to your reputation. You'll think that you have to hide it within yourself where it will continue to cause extensive damage.

We've seen this in the entertainment industry, where a large number of people attempt to access a limited number of roles. Unfortunately, those in control send out calls that put those seekers in compromising positions. Although some of the perpetrators are being canceled and even prosecuted today, the victims live with the pain from the incident. Although some victims have gone on to enjoy successful careers in the industry, they might be viewed as the "lucky ones." Countless others have crossed their integrity and didn't receive the opportunities they expected.

Your mind is a recorder and always on. When you act against your integrity, that act will affect your spirit. Although it may require a greater investment of time and energy, the effortless way eliminates the physical and psychological strings attached when you violate your life's codes of justice. Whenever we act in a way that we feel is wrong, the profit we gain from the action will never outlive the long-term spiritual effect the act created.

If you investigate your inner activity, you'll see it leading to the conditions in your world. We miss valuable learning opportunities when we don't discover our internal contributions to our lives. Our problem is that science is currently unable to test these internal movements. This activity occurs within, and there's currently no way to externally collect data for organized research. However, we all have the tools to conduct our own investigation. You know what you genuinely think, see, feel, and experience from within. You can assess life for yourself. You were born with this gift, but you have to learn to evaluate what you're experiencing.

Before we continue to struggle, we need to identify any resistance conflicting with our actions. We must decide if our understanding is unproductive and if we need to change, stop the activity causing the problem, or try to press forward. Sometimes, we become so stubborn in our understanding that we notice the difficulties our outlook creates, but we refuse to change. Unfortunately, we'll never question our view if we're not observing ourselves objectively. That makes it impossible to learn anything from our experiences. Instead, we'll keep wasting our energy in situations that we continue to subconsciously support.

You don't have to spend your life over-analyzing your inner activity. But you're not supposed to sit around and ignore your hidden impact. You should enjoy life! But you must observe yourself along the way. You shouldn't be able to name all the stars in the galaxy, every member of your favorite team, or every trait of your favorite celebrity, but unable to determine what's going on within you.

Discovering more about yourself ignites creativity and empowers you. Instead of waiting and reacting to calls, you learn to take the lead in your life. If you're resting in your dissatisfaction, you may not discover the opportunities to grow until life consistently thrusts situations to awaken you.

Awareness is the key to discovering and managing our presence. We never know what we will face on any given day, but we can control how we allow it to alter our state of being. Your internal activity determines the burden or ease you take from every situation. You are the determining factor that decides how everything impacts your being. Even minor events affect your presence in some way, and that alters your reality. Therefore, the only way to stay abreast of the continuous effect of the things touching you is to increase your inner awareness as you move through your daily activities.

You don't have to try to block things out or even attempt to control your thoughts. Instead, you can manage your moods and attitudes from what you observe and experience instead of reacting. That's the level of control given to us. But it's challenging to achieve and carry out daily. Diving into the credibility of your beliefs and your outlook will allow you to release many of the attachments that are tying you to some of your unpleasing habits and behaviors. You can't control what happens in the world. You can only manage how these experiences affect you spiritually.

When your views are tainted and obscured, they will have a negative impact. That effect will be displayed in your responses and the actions you take. But you have to take an unbiased perspective as you investigate your beliefs. You're the only one who can honestly assess yourself because you know what is occurring within. That's why you must deliberately monitor your state of being.

When you compromise your integrity, your conscious mind will pay the price. Though most of the world doesn't know the truth about your actions, the only world that genuinely matters knows the truth. That's the one that exists within yourself. It causes you to lose sleep at night. It never lets you forget the injustice you undertook. There will be a constant reminder that leads you into states of frustration. That frustration can be traced back to your questionable acts. When we find ourselves in this predicament, we have to abandon embarrassment, shame, or guilt and seek professional help. It might be difficult to forgive yourself, but you must let it go. The best way to move forward is to use it for the growth it offers you, but you may need help to see it.

Premium Alternatives

Chapter 20

Deceptive Vision

Emotionally Moved

Your internal activity can have a profound effect on everything. You can create barriers or pathways to success through your presence. When we experience fear or anxiety in stressful situations such as giving a speech, we're suffering from a self-created barrier. That barrier prevents us from the comfort and ease we would typically experience. That barrier is an example of something moving our spirit. It can't be measured, it can't be heard, and it can't be touched, but it's definitely felt. That feeling can negatively affect your speech, but it can also affect other areas moving forward.

A simple search on the Internet can also be a spark. While searching the web, you receive influence that personally impacts you. Instead of finding the answer you sought, you find yourself emotionally moved by what you've read. That movement may temporarily sidetrack you or completely alter your beliefs. Although you were searching for a simple answer, you answered a self-initiated call.

No one else can sense the activity occurring within you, but it exists. Others may be able to see the effects of the activity within your behavior, but the reason behind it was the way it touched your spirit. That's the reality of many things we do in life. Others witness the effects of our inner activity because our actions have internal sources; therefore, they're difficult to trace. If you want to discover the root of your actions, the origins of your reactions, and the foundation that must be adjusted before any change or transformation can occur, look at your inner activity. It lives behind every action.

We use this knowledge in many areas of life but forget to use it internally. When investigators search for motives, they look past the event to find a source for the action. Criminal investigations lead to origins such as jealousy, envy, rage, and greed. Those aren't physical attributes. Aren't those the results of inner turmoil from our view of external situations? Even when we search to discover the reasons behind the impressive things people accomplish, it's rarely rooted in physical activities. Their motivation may appear physical, but the motives behind their acts are always further than material gains. They may have trained for months or studied for years, but their inner commitment

214

sustained them. That commitment may have been created by a desire to impress someone, the pressure to prove something to someone, or the need to feel accomplished. Even a desire to help others satisfies a need that lives within. Motives come from the spirit, just as our desires do. Our awareness is essential to uncovering our unexplained attractions in life.

This inner activity can even suppress our logic, but it's often overlooked. When we're not observant, we even find ourselves momentarily aroused to do things totally against our character. That moment could make a substantial difference on our journey if we act on it. We believe we control our behavior with intellect but sometimes we make poor decisions that appear to be informed. When a caller comes along and whispers in our ear or sparks an emotion, we often lose sight of our objectives and follow the new feeling awakened within.

The things we're emotionally moved by can dominate our lives, so we must become aware of those attachments. When faced with choices, we consider the various factors involved; but our decisions heavily depend on our current state of being. That is part of what makes it so difficult to break our habits, including how we answer calls. The way we feel in the moment always plays a role in our actions. When we're uncomfortable, bored, or unsettled, we quickly return to the things that provide us a taste of comfort that we're familiar with. Science and medical evidence often prove that some of the practices we rely on for that comfort are unhealthy, yet we continue to pursue them. The overwhelming evidence from science can't overrule our desire in many cases. Our reasoning minds might know what's best, but that doesn't mean we'll automatically follow that path. Spiritual attractions such as habits and addictions can easily subdue logic.

When you look at the circumstances you encounter, you'll see how emotions and feelings initiate your activities. You could do something extraordinary or ill-advised; an unseen origin can always be identified. Even your impulse reactions come from the inner state you're operating from when you react. That state is heavily influenced by the thoughts we're allowing to dominate our presence. We have to be cautious of the influences we're accepting that are feeding our thoughts and emotions.

We credit our minds with the beautiful things we accomplish because we think before we act. But we think of many concepts and ideas we fail to act on. That may be because we aren't spiritually aligned with them. That isn't bad because we have negative thoughts that will lead to adverse actions if we automatically pursue them. The fact that we aren't attached to those ideas is beneficial. Yet, there are many concepts that we are connected to which lead to unproductive attitudes and behaviors. We can learn to recognize and internally address these aspects instead of becoming comfortable and allowing them to linger and escalate.

216

If we aren't aware of our essence, we'll consistently detach from our thoughts which could move us from concepts to actions in the areas we want to improve. We'll remain attached to what we're currently aligned with rather than transition to something greater. Or we'll remain trapped in our current cycle of answering the calls in ways that block positive interactions. When we become familiar with our spiritual relationship with life and move from a new perspective, we'll see how our actions align with our inner activity. When a call arrives that we aren't expecting, we'll be prepared to answer it with clarity.

Deceptive Vision

Mental images can deceive us if we're not careful. Sometimes, we believe what we see in the distance is the beauty we desire to experience. We build ourselves up with anticipation as we move towards it. Then, once we get closer or actually obtain it, we find it's not as we thought it would be.

When we see something we desire, we imagine ourselves experiencing it. We can't go on social media without viewing the beautiful lifestyles, material objects, awesome experiences, or novel ideas that others are sharing. Callers constantly provide us with impressions they want us to embrace. If we accept it, we place ourselves in the scene to create the feeling. When you create the image, you can always find sources that will support it, even if it's inaccurate. While working on obtaining it, we spiritually build up the feeling of how awesome it will be. Finally, when we capture it, the sensation of securing what we wanted overrides all other emotions. Eventually, we may find that what we sought to achieve was not as beautiful as the picture we painted. Or, it was as thrilling as expected, but it's simply unsustainable. Although the blame for the distorted visions we accept lies on us, we certainly had help creating them.

It may hit you immediately or take weeks, months, or even years. You find that the image you created has deceived you, and the reality of obtaining it doesn't measure up, or it doesn't last. Your sight is one of the best deceivers of fact. When you learn to create an authentic relationship with your vision, you can move past the false sense of wholeness you envision in the material world. You can manage your expectations and use them to guide your movements instead of allowing them to deceive and dominate you. Managing your expectations is a delicate practice because expectancy is a powerful source. But when our expectations are misguided, they cause us to invest inappropriately.

When deceptive callers approach, they're targeting your imagination. They can't force you to do as they want you to, but they can attempt to adjust your perception. Once your outlook changes to their perspective, you're more likely to move in their desired direction. Callers play a vital role in influencing our expectations. If we don't recognize the influence occurring, we'll suffer from the inaccurate vision we're relying on.

If You Can't See It

While inadequate visions can lead us astray, we still need to rely on our vision to move us to be better. Our vision helps guide us toward our goals, but sometimes, we have needs that appear out of reach, so we struggle to visualize them. We desire success but can't see ourselves realistically obtaining it. Our vision may have deceived us in the past, or we have a belief telling us we don't deserve it, so we refuse to develop the vision in our minds. Our attempts to pursue these goals will be frustrating because we don't seriously pursue goals that we can't relate to.

We know that success is possible because others have accomplished similar goals, but we don't feel it's available for ourselves. When we encounter setbacks towards our goal, abandoning it is easier when it hasn't internally moved to vision. That movement from idea to conception is critical. If it hasn't occurred, we suppress our goals and dreams before they can develop.

Our vision brings dreams to life. Dreams don't automatically activate. Something within you must propel your goals to vision. That transition is spiritual. Without consciously acknowledging this process, you'll depend on someone or something to inspire you. With awareness, you don't need external activity to inspire or spark your being. You shouldn't rely on inspiration to move you; it may never arrive!

It isn't easy to create a realistic vision when we don't have prior successful experiences in that area of our lives. If we were born into deprived circumstances and never truly experienced anything different, it might be hard to move past that state. The poor condition most people think of is financial, but underprivileged states exist in every area. We're all deprived in some areas, and life will continue to offer opportunities for growth in those areas.

If you were raised in an environment without positive transactions in a particular area, it might be challenging to move forward when you face difficulty in that area. For example, if you always had problems budgeting and suddenly received a fortune, it might be hard to sustain it because you don't have experience in that physical state. You might surrender your wealth to others who are aware of your condition and are looking to take advantage of it. Likewise, receiving love from someone when you aren't familiar with that kind of intimacy might make it hard to maintain a relationship because you don't know how to reciprocate. When we receive something contrasting with our norms in life, we might mishandle it because we've never seen ourselves thriving in that area.

Reality gives us insight into our true visions. The things we're seriously bonded with always appear in our actions because we subconsciously pursue them. We don't seriously pursue things we don't believe are natural for us. We may flirt with the idea for a while but eventually return to what we genuinely believe in.

We must learn to create a realistic vision of the success and wellness we seek before we attack them.

We shouldn't need to actually see something to experience it. We must develop the ability to create based on a vision we craft. We have to learn to participate in our spiritual navigation through life. It can propel us to act without relying on inspiration to move us. It's essential to overcome restrictive circumstances. We can't escape a harmful situation if we internally embrace it and accept it as the end. We can accept it as today's reality because it's real, but we must establish the spiritual intention to transition away from it. That's an activity that must occur internally.

Unfortunately, most of us aren't visualizing what we prefer to experience. Instead, we're imagining what we've accepted for ourselves. Then, we're using our lives to fulfill that accepted vision because it has become the only reality we trust and believe in. Callers also help us set our sights on their priorities. They want us to move in their preferred direction and deny our own.

Changing that vision becomes challenging when you're unhappy, unsatisfied, or need a transformation. You can't easily remove all the aspects of your current vision like deleting files on a computer. You've accepted and sustained those views to create your life. You can't unlearn the knowledge, beliefs, and experiences you've relied on to manage your life overnight. But you can decide to reposition and adjust your approach to anything. That requires a renewed relationship between the world you are experiencing and your interpretation of it. That renewal is a spiritual transformation. It subdues the restrictive enemy that dwells within.

You won't fully attempt to move toward a reality you don't believe is possible for you. If you grew up in poverty, it may be difficult to truly visualize yourself in better conditions. If you're running in a marathon, you're not completing it if you can't see yourself running to the finish line. If you're attending medical school, it will be harder to complete if you can't honestly see yourself as a doctor. If you're seeking wellness, you're not seriously committing to exercising if you don't see yourself as better than you are now. You may be able to start without the vision, but as you advance, it will either develop within you or you'll allow something to disturb your journey. That's a risk that causes too many goals and dreams to be terminated.

Some parents understand how crucial it is for their children to see and witness forms of success early in life. They are committed to showing their children great possibilities and ensuring they experience them. They introduce them to it, allow them to touch it, meet the people who have done it, and make a connection so they know it's real. You should adopt a similar routine to accept the reality of your dreams and turn them into visions. Although you don't need to literally see your desire to move towards it, whatever you can use to bring it to reality will be beneficial. Something as simple as writing down your vision can have a positive impact. Continuously repeating that every day as your world changes can further enforce your vision.

Witnessing an example of our vision shouldn't be necessary, although it can be helpful. We have to ensure we offer ourselves the best opportunity to improve our situation.

Premium Alternatives

Chapter 21

Love & Creativity

A Better Way

When you establish an optimistic vision, you can use it as your foundation. You might not be able to see or touch it today, but you're gaining on it or distancing yourself from it every day. Situations change by the minute as callers approach; you can keep pace by being flexible with your answers. Your chance for success in retaining focus depends on your ability to adjust your presence, not solely on completing the steps. The underlying reason behind your actions or failure to act is more important.

Our state of being is vital to the effort we plan to use in our actions. When it's time to act, we invoke a feeling that propels us. We might be excited, nervous, inspired, reluctant, or any combination of emotions regarding the activity we're engaging in. Our essence will power our effort in that activity, rightly or wrongly. Achieving better results in unfamiliar areas requires a renewed internal commitment before we act. We won't tap into our creativity when needed without a renewed inner agreement. We'll allow the situation to stop our progress. Our essence may have the most significant impact on our outcome in any situation. It initiates the energy that animates our actions. If we're not internally prepared, the best physical conditions won't lead us to success.

When we perform activities, we look at our results to judge our performance. The answers we need exist within the activity, not the results. We create results during the event, not at the finish line. But the finish line is where we focus our attention. We must learn to achieve results by creating attachments to the activities that lead to our desired results. The results help us identify our initial intent, but the actions that lead to the results show the internal agreements dominating us.

There are an unlimited number of ways to accomplish a task. We need to find and attach to the methods that we're most comfortable with. We must use our creativity to construct strategies that lead us to our goals instead of trying to repeat the common techniques others use. If we aren't loyal to the methods, we won't follow through with the actions that lead us to our goal. In a way, you must fall in love with the level of commitment that matches your goal and not the goal itself.

If we can't fall in love with the commitment that matches our goal, we must consciously lower it because we've already spiritually lowered it. That may seem counterproductive, but it may be the only way to progress toward our goal. We may not be prepared to lose fifty pounds by August, but we may be ready to lose five pounds over the next three weeks and move forward. It may not appear to be much, but a renewed perspective can carry us to the end, allowing us to stay the course.

The fact that you can't commit to the required actions to achieve the highest level of your goal is an indication. It's announcing that you aren't in love with that level of success. You have other commitments that surpass it. You likely can't see it as reality yet. You may be ready to commit to a lower level, which is fine. You only need to acknowledge that fact consciously, or you'll continue in a state of desire rather than a state of action. Desire without a personally realistic vision produces an immovable anchor to your current position.

Awareness offers the power to navigate any predicament and turn it into a valuable experience. When we mistakenly answer a call we shouldn't have, we have to adjust on the fly without allowing the error to subdue us. Life won't give us a time-out to get things together. We must escape the storms of life during the scenarios that arise. There isn't anything so overwhelming that we should run away from it. We can overcome any situation, achieve goals, and untie entanglements. Acknowledging and using our awareness is essential in controlling our actions and lives.

We must be prepared to navigate the forever-changing circumstances to establish and sustain our wellness. Things will continually change. If we continue to cling to our current understanding, our results will remain as they are. When we choose to live based on physical evidence, we often excuse the broader significance of our choices at the moment. Awareness allows you to discover and consciously use the internal presence that directs your actions.

Your focus on physical aspects cements you to your current circumstances. Your spirit is attached to your interpretation of success. You must ensure your desire matches your true belief in yourself. This is easier said than done because we assume that we always want the best possible results, but that's not always the truth.

Maybe you held back effort at times? Perhaps you were distracted by something that hampered your ability to focus. These internal reasons could cause you to stumble, but they don't appear as physical evidence. You only know that you smoked another pack of cigarettes, became angry instead of remaining calm, or watched TV instead of exercising.

If you don't exercise according to your schedule, that's a choice. If you don't study when necessary, that's also your decision. You know what you need to do to meet your verbalized goals, yet you may choose to neglect them.

On the surface, it appears that you decided to watch TV instead of exercise, but you really chose to deny your goal. That indicates that your goal doesn't align with your internal agreements. That conflict will appear in your world as a failure toward your goal, but it's rooted in your internal agreements.

The complex matters we face can't forcibly overwhelm us. We have to surrender our ability to navigate through them peacefully. Once we give up, we allow the circumstances to dictate our essence.

That is a terrible place to exist.

The issues we encounter don't tear us down; we allow them to dismantle us. We negatively interpret situations and allow that version to develop into our circumstances. Our actions and movements are rooted in this internal activity, manifesting as physical obstructions to our desired outcome.

But this manifestation comes from within.

Creativity is the tool that allows us to navigate through the trials of life with confidence. It's the perfect partner for spirituality. Creativity is the instrument that moves our vision from concept to reality. Proper use can provide you with anything. But its misuse can cost you everything, including your life. Understanding how to use your creativity will allow you to paint the Mona Lisa. Yet, the improper use will cause you to paint yourself into a corner of misery and desperation.

Creativity is a remarkable gift. It's the tool that can move you in an intentional direction. However, when you misuse it, you can distance yourself further from your desired destination. Weaving creativity with awareness is essential. It's the tool we use to carry out our internal agreements. When we know our agreements, we consciously use our creativity to align with them. When we don't know our established agreements, we instinctively use our creativity with them.

Creativity can be the difference in your level of success in any field. You'll see top athletes who gain success in college sports but fail to make it as a professional. It's easy to say they weren't good enough to make it, but that would be an incomplete assessment. Some collegiate athletes that aren't as talented as their counterparts compete in pro sports. They created a niche by finding a situation where their services could be an asset. They didn't wait for a call; they made a path for themselves. You can point to any industry to find the same situation. Some singers, actors, and entertainers in genres don't appear to be the greatest in their profession, yet they are profitable. They've used their creativity to carve out a place even though they might not seem the best. It may be a matter of opinion, but those opinions are all you need for success. Everyone doesn't have to agree on their ability.

You see it every day as well. Someone will use their creativity to get a promotion even though it seems they aren't qualified for it, yet they occupy the position. Creativity is available to everyone, but sometimes we misuse it. The most successful criminals in the world use the power of creativity every day. You have to use your awareness to stay alert to their actions, or they'll call upon you to become their next victim.

You can see the incredible means people use to take advantage of others by misusing their creativity. These criminals creatively devise intensive plans and schemes to deceive others. This misuse of imagination results in a negative situation. When using creativity, you must respect the rules of society. If not, you should prepare to face the consequences of misusing it.

Creativity is nature's app that levels the playing field of opportunities for everyone. It doesn't require any physical labor but requires a conscious effort to use it effectively. We already own one of the most valuable assets on the planet, but we give it up daily. We surrender it to others who recognize its value and have created means to exploit it for profit.

Premium Alternatives

Chapter 22

Awareness
in Results

When results from our actions don't equal our expectations and callers constantly separate us from our intentions, we need to consider our state of being. When we aren't settled in our environment, we don't need to focus on the problems in the world that are challenging us. Instead, we have to start where we are and look internally at our current state. Acknowledging our inner agreements and adjusting our state of being is vital.

There are always answers in our presence, but we must stay alert for them. We can look out to find external causes of the issues we're experiencing, and we'll always find some, but many of them are false. In reality, it's difficult to outperform the state of being we're currently residing in. We may successfully conceal our inner frustration for a while, but our essence will eventually present itself in the physical world.

If we're operating from a negative state, we shouldn't expect to experience results that exceed that state. People in sync with their presence can deliberately place themselves in a mindset to motivate or de-escalate in any situation. They see the vision they need to establish for a particular activity internally and adapt. Once completed, they pull themselves out of that state because it's no longer needed. We all do this at times when we're prepared and aware of what to expect. We know from experience the essence we need to obtain for success in certain circumstances, and we create it. Moving forward, we must learn to use that awareness when life sends calls we aren't expecting. We can amplify that ability by increasing our presence.

Your external demeanor is valuable, but recognizing your internal state is essential. It's important in discovering creativity that most can only dream about. As a result, we can obtain levels of satisfaction that we've never experienced. Although it would be nice, we don't obtain bliss and remain there without interruption. Instead, we need to be present and prepared to adjust to find the best outcome. This is how we can maintain our maximum level of creativity regardless of the situation. Instead of allowing ourselves to become victims of the stressful circumstances that arise, we become the leader.

Genuine Concern

When someone greets you with concern, they're usually referring to how your day is going or how you're feeling. Maybe the more important question to ask others is, "Where are you spiritually?" You can recognize hints of where someone is spiritually by their outward appearance, but you can never actually know where they are from the outside. They can deceive you with their external presentation, but the truth exists internally.

We can deceive others by painting a pleasant external picture when we're really in a terrible place. As a result, we won't receive the support we need because of our ability to conceal the truth. Of course, we can always fool others, and we can even fool ourselves. But the basis of a solid spiritual foundation is never to let that happen.

There isn't anything you do that isn't affected by your spiritual state. It is your foundation. You can spend your life training for an event, then fail at it simply because you're not spiritually engaged when it's time to perform. Most of us don't consciously carry our inner activity into other areas of our lives because we don't recognize the process. We're simply going through the motions of what we normally do. We need to step back and notice the spiritual effect in our lives because most of us are using it subconsciously. When we awaken our awareness, we can begin to consciously apply it to every area of our lives.

Premium Alternatives

Part Five

Better Impact

Chapter 23

Better Investing

Would you invest in something that's guaranteed to lose value?

Not only invest in it but return to it and create a habit?

That's what we do in many situations in our lives. We attach to things that aren't serving us. Then we continue to repeat the action. We must determine exactly what we're doing and see how it's affecting our lives. We can't assume we're doing the right things leading to our wellness. We must be sure of how things affect us. The challenge is to set aside the physical activities and focus on the inner activity leading the way.

Many things we do are necessary, but our approach to them may be detrimental. Are the approaches you're using preventing you from reaching your goals? Investigating yourself is the best way to transition from where you are to achieving the wellness you need.

Nothing can force you to move away from your goal, even with continuous distractions. You realize you have options. Your choices will separate you from your desired outcome or bring them into reality. They also send you back to unproductive habits instead of creating beautiful ones. Your self-inventory will show how you develop avenues to things you genuinely want. It will also show how you contribute to situations you don't desire. Either way, you're the power that controls your progress. We fall short in our self-assessment when we take a shallow look at ourselves. We know what we should desire, but we have to dive deeper to discover what we're chasing every day. That's where we'll find what's passionately moving us instead of what we think we're striving for.

Controlling Your Aim

Just because you haven't reached a goal doesn't mean you're a hostage to your environment and unable to break free. We go throughout our entire day shaping our lives. Surprisingly, we wonder why things turn out as they do, as if we had no part in it. Distractions don't consume us. We voluntarily engage in them and remain attached to them by choice. If we research our own lives the way marketers do, we will see the true power we possess. We wouldn't blame anyone else for our shortcomings. We must cherish the responsibility of directing our lives from within.

Others may give advice based on what they think you can achieve. We can't allow them to limit our possibilities. We must be self-aware. The best awareness is spiritual. You have to answer yourself. No one else can answer for you.

When you have a goal, you have to lock into it. You must weed out the actions that keep you from achieving what you want. Your thoughts are powerful, but you only act against your desire when you move. Thoughts can't act. You are the actor. When you're not in line with reaching your outcome, thoughts might arise that are against your goal. When you're focused on your desired outcome, you won't act on those thoughts. You recognize them as unproductive and won't allow them to create undesirable actions. We want all our creative efforts to move us toward our desires, not against them.

Remember that we're always creating. Make sure that your minute-to-minute creations are leading to your desired result. All other actions are against it. There's noise all around, fighting for our attention. Everything is a struggle for it. It drives the economy, keeps businesses alive, and is one of your greatest assets. The fight in business, entertainment, investing, and employment is for your attention. If they don't grasp your attention, businesses become irrelevant. When you acknowledge the importance of your attention, you understand its power in life.

When you decide to pay attention to something, it costs you more than the money you invest. The actual cost is the diversion from moving in the direction that you wish to move in. That's the overall cost of giving your attention. You invest in something that you didn't intend. That causes you to lose focus on your goal. When you drift from your aim, you travel somewhere that someone created for you, and that's how life flows. You must learn to navigate this world of attention, or you'll drift along instead of arriving at your chosen destination. You'll continue to help others in realizing their dreams instead of reaching your own.

You must begin to live more on your terms. You already know what has your attention, so you must determine if it's positively creating for you. You don't have to stop living and enjoying life. You don't have to stop enjoying the beauty of others' creations. But you must become aware of what you're investing in. Those investments determine where you are in your life. You can easily adjust by monitoring your investments if you ever desire to change. Then, you won't struggle to go from where you are to where you want to be. Acknowledging your spiritual nature will allow it to guide you and prevent it from being led by external influences.

You spread your influence onto others every day, although it may not be apparent that you do. Some people in your world allow you to affect their lives even though they may not freely admit it. They might not even recognize your effect on their thoughts and actions. We like to think we control our lives, but we don't look beneath the surface to see others moving us. Your position as an influencer in other people's lives is an important responsibility.

Although it's an individual's obligation to be aware of who or what may influence their life, most people don't know. They'll allow others to guide them away from their true desires. They won't understand why they aren't achieving their goals. So, as a father, mother, sister, coworker, neighbor, supervisor, or whatever role you play, you're influencing many others. You need to be aware of the lives you're touching. You're touching more people through influence than you'll ever physically touch throughout your life. For most people, that non-physical touch is more potent than anything physical.

Better Impact

Chapter 24

The Only Impartial Perspective

Society demands that we receive an education designed to prepare us for life. Yet, when completed, many of us aren't prepared to manage ourselves within the roles awaiting us. As a result, the economy soars while those contributing to it struggle to manage life's experiences.

Inner awareness is the overlooked aspect that allows us to navigate through life's demands with presence. Often, we struggle to deal with our reality when we lose finances, when friends and loved ones turn away from us, or when bad decisions come back to haunt us. We must be able to determine if the approach we're currently using is moving us toward solutions or merely pondering over the problem. Are we expecting a confrontation or a peaceful encounter? If we look without prejudice, we'll find ourselves acting in agreement with our expectations. We might make excuses to explain some of our actions, but that doesn't matter. An unbiased look will show how our activities guide us to our expectations.

When we view the core of any circumstance, we can only expect success or failure from within. The activities in the situation may cloud our ability to see our expectations, but our expectations are guiding our effort. We're internally building ourselves up for what we're genuinely assuming. It's showing up through our mindset, attitude, and actions. The activity brewing within is spiritual. That essence will affect the outcome through our actions. We omit that factor when we solely contribute success to hard work and only look at the numbers from scientific studies. There are many unseen factors contributing to our ability to work hard. When you can't see success, that perspective can affect your movements. There are unlimited reasons that we can't see success for ourselves. A spiritual foundation helps us discover these contributors so we can address them.

That's a tangible piece of spirituality from a human point of view. It flows from our expectations, then moves to an internal build-up preparing for what we expect. We'll find ourselves acting based on our expectations when we're observant. We may not have created the issues we face, but our actions will affect where we end. We'll dramatically affect how the scenario plays out moving forward. Our responses spring from our inner feelings about the situation and how it touched us. The result of that activity will be displayed through our actions.

The challenge is to remove clutter to discover our genuine outlook. That outlook is what we're attaching to our spiritual energy. The average person has many influences tossed before them every day. Those influences can alter your ability to see clearly. When it's time to react to something affecting your circumstances, you may not respond clearly. When you find yourself in one of life's many transitions, your ability to handle the weight will be challenged.

Others may say they understand, but they can't see it exactly as you do. They may have experienced the same situation you are experiencing, but no one interprets conditions in the same manner because we are all unique. That's why you must discover spirituality and its effect on your life.

Our inner activity affects everything we encounter. That explains the powerful impact of spirituality. If we set a negative foundation, we won't look for positive opportunities to manage our situations. These opportunities confront us every day. As each one approaches, we're too busy pondering the negative state to recognize the opportunities passing by.

When someone improves their life, they make changes they possibly could have made at any stage. They had to decide to accept a different way forward. Our awareness offers a unique perspective with solutions. If we aren't constantly questioning our outlook, we're missing chances to adjust it to improve our circumstances.

Are we expecting a phone call with a solution or one that carries us deeper into the predicament? Do you think that expectation is altering your movements? How can we expect to recognize the answer if it shows up when we're spiritually focused on the problem? How can we allow room for answers to develop when we aren't mentally prepared to recognize possible solutions when they appear? If we're spiritually building ourselves up to explode, are you really looking to resolve anything, or has the ego taken control?

The same person delivering bad news to us probably has answers to assist us. But, to take advantage of the possibility, we must be able to adjust our demeanor. Living from the idea that we're drowning in our issue is very different than living with the attitude of emerging from it. Although the facts are the same, living from a renewed outlook opens our awareness to opportunities to resolve our issues rather than sulking in despair or brewing in anger.

What we agree on spiritually will eventually appear physically through our actions. If you're moving with hesitancy, fear, or anger, the effect of those temperaments will show up in your results. Others may mistakenly believe you're in total control of your situation because of your masquerade, but the way you're spiritually moving matters. Someone can display confidence externally but could genuinely be operating in fear. On the other hand, someone who appears timid could be the most prepared and confident internally. You can judge by appearances, but many times you'll be wrong.

Life is always challenging us to approach everything with presence. Learning to remove yourself from circumstances is crucial. That offers you the chance to eliminate actions that may intensify the problem. Viewing from an overall perspective is critical, so the events and conditions you're experiencing won't negatively influence your judgment. Presence removes the circumstances and allows you to focus on your overall well-being.

The spirit we bring impacts our outcome because it always energizes our attitude and actions. You may find yourself fighting with others that you can't change, battling with circumstances you don't have the power to change, or battling internally with yourself. Our ability to control any situation starts with the spiritual essence we bring to the scenario.

Two Unique Worlds

There are always two worlds occurring in your life.

There's the world we're all collectively experiencing with its material and ideological aspects. It offers the shared experience we live. But there's also the individual outlook of the world, which we experience from within. That's the world callers attempt to access when reaching out to you. Identifying these two worlds is a vital step in developing our awareness.

These two worlds consist of our internal view of life and the world that exists externally. That external world refers to everyone outside of you, even those with intimate contact with you. Although it would be convenient for these two worlds to be exactly the same for everyone, that isn't the case. Your inner world doesn't mirror anyone else's, which is vital to remember as we interact with others.

The most crucial world is the one you internally experience. It guides your interactions with the external world. You can't navigate the outer world accurately without a thorough and clear understanding of your view. However, when you know yourself from within, you can confidently navigate the external world when things don't go as you'd prefer. You will never master life, but you can always gain more understanding from your encounters.

When challenged to overcome issues in the world, you must consider the two aspects we all experience. Many have overcome components of the external world by finding success in business, entertainment, politics, or some other area of worldly power, yet they still suffer despite their success.

Do you ever wonder how someone in the most challenging situation can remain calm and maintain a sense of peace? Yet, on the other hand, do you see how something which appears to be trivial can tear someone apart? When things don't transpire as desired externally, you can't allow them to disrupt the primary world within. Your awareness enables you to maintain peace amid the worst trials. It also permits you to maintain control of your world even when it appears to others that they somehow have control of you. That's the importance of understanding the two worlds we all encounter. Elevating the external world and allowing it to dominate can lead to a desperate, deflated, confused, or volatile essence.

Many people have allowed themselves to place the external world ahead of their existence. You can't allow yourself to become a victim of the world by downplaying the importance of your existence. You can easily allow yourself to be tossed about and dismissed as irrelevant, allowing that view to lead to inappropriate actions. Some understand this priority, but they incorrectly apply it to material aspects. Your priority must transition to the importance of your spirit. That understanding limits the power of greed, envy, and rage that dominates a physical focal point.

When you prioritize your inner world, you won't allow yourself to be dismissed, regardless of your current position. You can create miracles for yourself and the world only when you recognize your relevance. The world doesn't owe you anything, but you owe yourself everything spiritually. That's why you must understand the priority your inner world requires. This stance isn't based on arrogance, ego, or selfishness. It's the opposite of these characteristics, but it places your spirit at a level of importance that the world will never acknowledge.

If you fail to prioritize your spiritual existence, you won't consider the unlimited opportunities available. You could be the president of a nation or homeless; your spiritual wellness should always be your highest priority.

We get so caught up in the material world that we don't acknowledge the aspects that internally animate our experiences. We have thoughts, feelings, and emotions but shrug them off. These are elements that reveal our current spiritual state. We might see them as irrelevant annoyances, but that's a huge mistake. We must acknowledge that they play a leading role in our self-awareness. Learning to recognize them is essential for our well-being. Maneuvering things you can physically touch is easy. Learning to grasp an aspect you can't physically manipulate is an entirely different level of our human experience.

There will always be things occurring that are outside of our control. With a solid spiritual foundation, the world could crumble around us, and we wouldn't panic. We'd understand that circumstances don't control our being unless we let them, and we'd maintain stability. We might get caught up in the moment, but we'll collect ourselves when we return to the spiritual foundation that centers us in any scenario.

At times, we feel helpless because of our circumstances. We react irrationally by fighting, running, hiding, threatening, misjudging, and other unproductive means of answering calls. We use these means that cause us to miss opportunities for positive interactions. A strong spiritual foundation prevents us from allowing events and circumstances to impact our responses to calls. When life requires us to make a transition, we can accept it. We continue moving forward with our lives. We won't feel we're at our wit's end with nowhere to turn. We won't accept that the world is caving in on us.

When spiritually grounded, we find creative ways to move forward when the circumstances could lead to destruction. When we face transitions in life, the events can propel us or cause us to shut down. We might not have a problem moving forward if the change is favorable. However, when unfavorable, we sometimes find it hard to move ahead. In addition to dealing with our situation, we must continue to deal with life. Without inner awareness and a firm foundation, the circumstances and events of life can easily overwhelm us.

Knowing we have a spiritual impact, we realize we must move on. It's never the end of the world. How many failed lottery winner stories must we witness to learn this lesson? Sometimes, the story of events that so many people desire ends tragically. They receive the prize, then eventually find themselves broke, lonely, or worse. In many of these situations, we experience an inner conflict because we failed to adjust spiritually. We all struggle to deal with transitions, even when considered favorable.

We can't evade the problems that approach us in life. However, spiritual awareness will help guide us through. Without it, you'll remain in an uncomfortable state of being. You'll feel you're unable to uplift yourself. If you become overwhelmed by the scenario, you'll dwell in it because of your inability to move, not because there aren't alternatives.

When you develop a spiritual outlook, you'll recognize the status of the transition you're experiencing and adjust. Your familiarity with yourself will determine how long it will take to adjust. You can't escape life. Spiritual awareness helps you get through the transition. You release the feeling that you're frozen and realize you can advance.

Most of us haven't developed a broad vantage point of our lives in the present tense. Even fewer consider the impact we can have before we move a muscle. We don't look at the current situation with the understanding that it's manageable. It's only a piece of our greater existence. We haven't learned to take an alternate view. Instead, we dwell within our scenarios and overreact.

We choose to focus overly on the crisis that's in front of us. While it's true that we must confront the things facing us, we must also understand that these issues are manageable. We shouldn't jump into panic mode and react to that overwhelming feeling we're experiencing.

The pressure of dealing with our issues can be overwhelming. We forget that today's problems always strengthen us for tomorrow. Always! We allow today's activity to crush us instead of allowing it to evolve and develop into wisdom and experience. We can consciously decide to let that happen or fight and hope we eventually get it. Spiritual awareness doesn't necessarily mean we have a calm or pleasant demeanor in every situation. This awareness allows our reactions to come from our consciously selected state of being. We stop answering calls from unproductive states such as fear, hopelessness, and anger. We evolve.

Chapter 25

Authentically Compelling

If you continually yield to how things are, how can you progress in any area of life?

More importantly, if you always submit to other people's will, how do you expect to spiritually grow when spirituality is a personal interaction with life?

If you see yourself as irrelevant (as others will allow you to do), how can you exceed the current level you've accepted?

There can't be a spiritual uplifting if you yield to the inadvertent boundaries you've affirmed. You won't discover a way to elevate yourself and the world if you can't visualize and acknowledge yourself as compelling. That's how you begin to uplift yourself spiritually.

The world can't realize the potential for greatness in you until you notice it yourself. You don't have to be great in anyone else's eyes, but you must be excellent in your own. Being great is a personal experience you can achieve on any level. You can be great at your career, relationships, or wherever you choose.

There isn't a pass-or-fail line in life. No one can label you a failure or a success with any validation because success is immeasurable. You set your own bar, and only you know if you're successful in achieving your actual goals. Some may look at your situation and label you successful in their eyes. However, if you don't reach your desired result, their opinion doesn't mean anything. Others may claim that you failed, but if what they consider failing was not your goal, you didn't fail. You set your own bar in life, and no one can judge your success, though they will. The important point to remember is the growth available from the experience.

Accepting opinions causes so many problems that shouldn't exist. One of life's most valuable gifts is the ability to refuse to accept negative opinions. No one can force you to invest in their opinion. You have to give up your right to deny a view that can influence you. You have the choice to either refuse it or accept what's offered. Whatever you allow will affect you spiritually. Others may judge you based on one shortcoming, but you shouldn't buy it.

Some people believe that when things are going well in one area of life, everything else falls into place. But we're never free of other areas of life because we've succeeded in one area. Financial success only guarantees financial security. Fame and popularity only account for those specific areas. We must remain aware of our spiritual position in all facets of life. Overall spiritual well-being ensures peace with any aspect of life as it approaches. Acknowledging your spiritual nature is the only way to prepare for any situation. No one can call you a failure, but if you believe you are one, you may begin to act like one. You are always impacting life, and that effect never ends.

Better Impact

Chapter 26

Marketing to Yourself

When you view a clip or television episode, you may see the same advertisement repeated several times. You realize you're being fed something someone wants you to engage in. That's a form of marketing we must use for our wellness. We must find ways to feed ourselves spiritually.

We often find ourselves setting goals and making resolutions but unable to stick with them. One reason is that we don't have our own marketing team promoting our goals back to us. Everyone is selling what they want us to see and experience. We must use methods to reduce these distractions and boost our own intentions.

Meditation can be essential in establishing input in our world. It can help offset the crowding from the endless external influences. We don't have to label it as meditation, just designated time to escape the noise and promote wellness. We use it to ensure our health remains a priority in our life.

If we don't learn to prioritize what we want for ourselves, we will continue to experience what others want us to encounter. We'll continue to follow the patterns of life that have been laid out for us. We'll continue to view the world others have painted for us. Therefore, we must become excellent self-marketers. We can't allow our desires to be disregarded by messages others have for us.

We already have forms of meditation we use every day, but we don't stop to acknowledge them. If we observe, we'll find ourselves pondering things, spending moments in deep thought, and reflecting on situations in our lives. Those moments have a spiritual effect on our presence. The results from these moments will also show up in our actions. If they're based on negativity, that can also expand in our lives.

We can meditate in a crowd or in seclusion. The activity is within you. People create their own forms of meditation, and whatever works to move your spirit is the correct method. When you meditate, you're consciously creating moments that relieve stress and re-introducing your presence that you may have abandoned.

Chapter 27

The Key to Transformation

Changing our habits rarely leads to permanent change, although it can offer temporary relief. Changing habits could spark an inner transformation, but it won't sustain it. A change in spirit solidifies our actions, introducing new thoughts, beliefs and an unyielding presence. That spiritual change must be our target. It moves us from thinking about taking desirable steps to performing them in the moment. It's the place we begin a promising movement, but it could also be the place we move in a detrimental or undesirable direction. But we choose to keep things as they are as we refuse to change our answers to life's calls. Therefore, we remain in the cycle we've become comfortable with.

Your awareness can alert you to what you're doing that isn't in your best interest and guide you away. It magnifies your senses by providing a point of view that isn't mentally or physically consumed by the situation. It doesn't allow ego, arrogance, or vanity to negate your options in any predicament.

Many of the problems we see unfolding in our lives are related to this scenario. We allow an otherwise controllable situation to inflate into something that did not have to exist. We allow the character associated with the role we're playing to override our ability to reason. That creates an uprising that is extremely difficult to diminish. Words will be delivered that can't be erased, actions will be taken that can't be redone, and relationships may come to an end. Greater awareness of our being will allow us to limit the ego that the mental and physical domination feed. Then the unprejudiced spirit can lead or at least provide a calming voice.

These encounters cause us to release our goals and objectives or accept the pressure to achieve them. They cause us to step away from being who we are and transition to a different being. These encounters become the opportunity that derails progress or the spark that leads to success. We expect them to be huge events, but they're often minor incidents that move us along our path. That's why they are so potent. Although we're alert for major encounters, minor incidents move us without warning.

Throughout life's days, weeks, and months, we reaffirm our inner agreements through our thoughts and actions. We move forward without understanding that our agreements are the key to any change or transformation we wish to achieve. If we stopped to observe our situations, we would find that it's easier to stick with our current agreement than create a new one. It's true even if our present circumstances are unwanted, uncomfortable, unhealthy, or dangerous. That's why we find it so hard to break habits. Instead of changing, we return to those handy habits when we respond to the situations we face.

If we looked at our day sincerely, we would find ourselves attached to our familiar scenarios by our prearranged agreements. When things proceed as planned, we comfortably move along with the sequence of events. However, we always react harmoniously with our established agreements when something beyond our control occurs. They set the foundation for our life as we approach everything we encounter. They are our primary influence guiding us through our everyday interactions.

Our agreements with life always dictate the direction we're moving. If you fail to consciously set up arrangements that connect your vision to the activities of life, it won't be easy accomplishing your goals.

Willfully ignoring your agreements leads to frustration, anxiety, and depression, but the source may not be apparent. One of our primary tasks in transforming our lives is to discover our agreements with life. Many of them aren't consistent with the contracts and goals we've consciously set for ourselves. Tracing them will help display the path that led you to your current situation. Ignoring your established agreements leads to confusion and discontent. If we don't acknowledge these agreements we've developed, we will continue to move in chaos.

If you want to live in peace, you must agree to maintain peace regardless of life's circumstances. If you wish to remain faithful to a particular religion, you must agree to keep the principles required by your faith. Even if you desire to live in turmoil, you must agree to invite it into your presence to ensure you experience it as often as possible. If we don't know our agreements, how will we know when we aren't traveling on the right road? We'll go out into the world and allow the circumstances and issues we encounter to dictate our lives.

Not knowing your agreements is like working a job that hasn't clearly stated your roles and responsibilities. You're moving along with your day performing tasks that you think are helpful but could be detrimental to the company's success. From your perspective, you're performing tasks that you've learned from your previous work experiences that seem to be appropriate. Then you receive data that shows your production is below standard. How can you meet a standard that you

268

don't even know exists? When you don't know exactly what your agreements are, you're moving in line with what you think is your desire but is actually satisfying a prior established agreement that you aren't aware of. Like your production at a job, your results are producing frustration and confusion because you think your actions are leading you toward your goals, but they're not.

Though you may not be aware that you've created agreements, you're subconsciously living in step with them. That's why we must invite awareness into our being. It allows us to discover the deals we've established that can explain our successes, failures, and discomfort. Sometimes, we're successful in an area, but we don't know the truth behind the success. We might falsely attribute it to our hard work, but there's always something behind the push through those complex tasks. Discovering that agreement is the key to your growth and expansion in other areas.

Where Are You Guiding Us?

We believe our purpose in life is something we must discover, but as we move along trying to identify or fulfill this purpose, we continue to affect life in the present tense. While pursuing our purpose, we're ignoring the effect we employ daily. Thus, we limit our conscious input of the power we currently possess. Most of us aren't famous and don't have a large social media presence, so mistakenly we minimize our impact. When you tune out your influence, regardless of how minimal it may seem, you're living without regard for the actual value of your life. You aren't acknowledging that everything you do has an effect. You're likely excusing any of your unproductive actions because you don't feel you're causing a huge impact on life. You may also be discounting the positive impact you're applying because you don't always see every residual effect.

That limited vision prevents us from seeing the total impact we have. It goes beyond our ability to trace it. We understand how we affect the environment by tossing a plastic bottle in the ocean, but we'll never be able to track the total effect of what we say and do to others throughout one day. As you begin to tally your days, you may start to scratch the surface of the impact of your presence. Then, you should start to see the resounding influence one life holds. You might view your effect abstractly, but the impact you project is a fact and is as concrete as any other scientifically provable aspect of life.

Recognizing the facts in life is always essential, but disregarding the intangible aspects that influence our lives is a disaster. We tend to ignore things that don't provide physical evidence, yet the lack of material evidence is the basis of spirituality. We must heighten our spiritual awareness to find that evidence. Everything that provides proof of existence doesn't require any human intervention to sustain them. Their physical presence confirms them. We must gain an understanding of our spiritual nature to identify other aspects that are affecting our lives. Learning how spirituality moves us can be revealing in understanding our current predicaments and how to move forward.

Spirituality begins with our inability to verify things with material evidence. It doesn't mean you ignore the physical laws of nature. However, you don't allow the lack of physical evidence to limit your awareness. That prevents progress in any research. In science, it would be difficult to advance to the unknown without a hypothesis, which, in essence, is a conscious leap of faith. Albert Einstein even spoke of the 'intuitive mind' as a sacred gift. The technology of tomorrow is untouched today but will be a fact tomorrow. Scientists have to lean on their awareness and knowledge to bridge today with tomorrow. It would help if you learned to use a similar technique. Your inner awareness relies on your senses but can advance beyond them.

The world is heavily influenced by the things we touch, see, and hear, yet we move with this undetectable presence that affects everything we experience. It's not a physical force, yet it plays a key role and impacts our physical world. We've learned to manage our lives with intelligence, personality, appearance, and physical strength. But life also touches us spiritually. Until we recognize this presence in every part of life, we will continue to face our struggles with an incomplete understanding.

Regardless of what you do with your life, you are serving a purpose. You may have lofty goals, or you may not desire to accomplish anything. Either way, you still have a purpose that you fulfill every day. You were born to move the world, and you do it involuntarily. So, where are you taking it? You can look at what you do daily and summarize your impact, but that's an incomplete assessment. The words you say, the ideas you cherish, and the things you do have a more profound effect than the current moment. As situations approach that seem intense, overwhelming, and consuming, remember that life is calling you with an opportunity to contribute through your response.

May You Discover the Peace That Life Has Reserved in Your Name Today

www.ingramcontent.com/pod-product-compliance
Lightning Source LLC
Chambersburg PA
CBHW032052020426
42335CB00011B/296